The A Imperative:

Empowering Instructors & Students

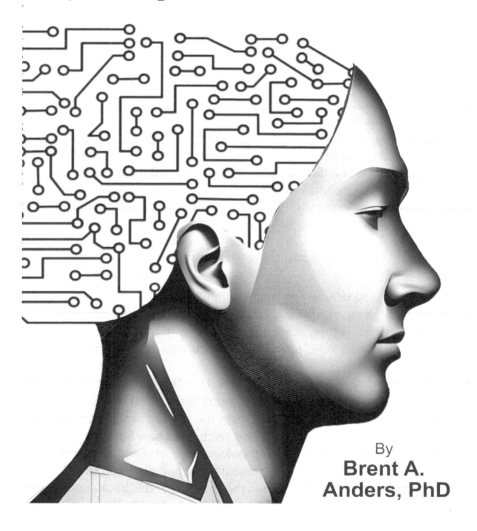

By
**Brent A.
Anders, PhD**

The AI Literacy Imperative:
Empowering Instructors & Students

By Brent A. Anders, PhD.

ISBN: 9798394372919

Keywords/Tags: AI Literacy, AI, Artificial Intelligence, ChatGPT, education, learning, teaching, awareness, knowledge, capability, critical thinking, overreliance, ethics, future, academic integrity, writing, prompts, guardrails, skills, soft skills, power skills, instruction, classroom

Cover Art Description: Book title "ChatGPT AI in The AI Literacy Imperative: Empowering Instructors & Students" along with author name: Brent A. Anders, PhD. The main image consists of the stylized profile of a human head with circuits coming out of it. This symbolizes how humanity has now become deeply connected with technology in general and AI specifically. Note that this book cover also represents how humans need to properly work together with AI as was done in the creation of this book cover image (done partially through AISEO Art AI image generation tool).

Sovorel Publishing, Edu. Blog
www.sovorelpublishing.com | www.youtube.com/@sovorel-EDU/videos

The AI Literacy Imperative:
Empowering Instructors & Students

TABLE OF CONTENTS

Acknowledgments

Special thanks to my many university friends and colleagues (professors, other faculty, librarians, and other staff), my other friends and colleagues on Twitter, YouTube, and LinkedIn from whom I have learned so much as we all work to continue to develop our AI Literacy. I am thankful for the opportunity and technology that allows us to come together to develop a human community of inquiry to work together to help one another and all of academia as it enters this new age of AI.

Additionally, a special thank you to my beautiful family, Nelli, Eva, and Lileth, for supporting me while I developed this book. I would also like to acknowledge and thank the readers of this book: teachers, professors, general instructors, students, and librarians for putting forth the effort to professionally develop their skills and capabilities to be better teachers and better able to directly prepare students for the new world around them. Finally, and as always, a special thank you to my Lord and savior Jesus Christ.

Foreword

Artificial Intelligence (AI) has evolved and continues to develop at an increasing pace, transforming how we interact with technology, education, businesses, and even ourselves. With the release of ChatGPT into the public on November 30th, 2023, and subsequent public AI tools such as Microsoft Bing Chat, and Google tools (Bard), and many more, the world has moved into a new era of enhanced capability that will forever change our future. All of us must be ready to use AI effectively/properly and to prepare our students as well.

As the director of a university's center for teaching and learning as well as a university lecturer and educational AI researcher, I have seen firsthand the impact that AI has had on education, both on instructors and in students. AI is changing how we think about and conduct education and will continue to play a critical role in shaping our future in many different ways.

However, as AI becomes more integrated into everyone's daily lives, it is a vital imperative that we develop a deeper understanding of its capabilities, limitations, and potential implications. This is where *AI literacy* comes in because everyone needs to have at least a basic understanding of these new AI technologies. It is an imperative.

In this book, based on research journals, news articles, interactions with instructors around the world, and my own academic experiences, I provide a comprehensive guide to AI literacy to include fully describing each component and identifying different techniques that can be used to teach it to students both online and/or face-to-face. Although this book is geared towards higher education, the information can be applied to lower education levels, the corporate world, and even military instruction. These AI literacy components will cover aspects dealing with a broad range of areas regarding the understanding of the world around us, implementation practices, safety/security, and ethical considerations.

My ultimate goal with this book is to equip you the instructor (instructional designer, student, or even librarian) with the knowledge and skills necessary to navigate the increasingly evolving landscape of AI and to harness its power to enhance your capabilities (and ultimately your students' capabilities/skills) for positive development and success.

The AI Evolution/Revolution

The release of ChatGPT on November 30th, 2022 by OpenAI was truly a revolution in that it marked the first time that the general public was able to directly interact with an advanced AI (Kay, 2023). A public that didn't need any coding knowledge, didn't need to get on a special waiting list, or pay any type of fee to access the AI that they were able to interact with by typing in questions in simple conversational English. ChatGPT became accessible to virtually anyone and everyone around the world. Since ChatGPT's release, many other AI's have become available, both from big companies like Google, as well as from many smaller companies, and companies like Microsoft that are using components of ChatGPT's AI language model: GPT4 (GPT: General Pretrained Transformer).

Yet the ability for all to access and use an advanced AI using a large language model (LLM) isn't the only revolution that has occurred. AI like ChatGPT, has started a revolution within education in that students can now easily learn directly from an AI as well as quickly and with minimal effort complete many different types of homework, take home tests and assignments. Naturally, many instructors have panicked at the thought of all students now able to easily cheat on any assignment and test.

This has caused a revolution of sorts in that now more instructors are realizing that they need to create better assignments and not only do high stakes summative assessments, but instead also do multiple formative assessments throughout the semester. There is also the issue of helping students use the AI appropriately as opposed to an easy downward path toward academic dishonesty. Additionally, many instructors are realizing that they aren't the sole-source of information or the gatekeepers of knowledge since AI like ChatGPT can answer virtually any type of question.

Many instructors are evolving in understanding that the main role of the teacher is to help students understand while developing a personal relationship, a community of learning to better motivate students (relevancy), make an emotional connection to the topic, aid in their reflection, and provide opportunities for application of new skills learned. Use of AI does not have to be an all-or-nothing endeavor in the classroom, but to make that choice we must understand it.

AI like ChatGPT has also now allowed for new ways of teaching and learning.

"Education is going to have to change"

The phrase "Education is going to have to change," is a somewhat famous/infamous line given by OpenAI founder (developer of ChatGPT) and CEO Sam Altman during an interview with ABC News' reporter, Rebecca Jarvis (ABC News, 2023). The conversation went as follows:

> **Rebecca Jarvis:** "How should schools be integrating this technology in a way that doesn't increase cheating that doesn't increase laziness among students?"

> **Sam Altman:** "*Education is going to have to change* but it's happened many other times with technology. When we got the calculator the way we taught math and what we tested students on, that totally changed. The promise of this technology, one of the ones that I'm most excited about, is the ability to provide individual learning. Great individual learning for each student. You're already seeing students using ChatGPT for this in a very primitive way to great success."

Sam Altman's answer was a bit nonchalant "education is going to have to change," and his analogy of the calculator doesn't seem to be quite the same as the magnitude that AI like ChatGPT now offers regarding what students can do with it. Yet, he isn't wrong.

The development of advanced AI will force education to change and hopefully improve. Sure some schools can try to ban it, but that is a band-aid approach that will ultimately fail. It will fail in being fully enforceable and it will fail the students by not properly preparing them for the new realities of a world that is full of AI. In another interview, Sam Altman expressed how AI like ChatGPT will start to affect virtually all jobs resulting in many more people needing to know how to use AI in order to remain relevant in the workforce (Fridman, 2023).

AI Literacy is now an imperative as it has become the new must have power/soft skill that all must possess in order to best compete in the new rapidly developing business world. Groups and representatives from around the world such as the European Union (EU), United Nations Educational, Scientific and Cultural Organization (UNESCO), World Economic Forum, Massachusetts Institute of Technology (MIT), and Forbes have all expressed the vital need for all to develop AI literacy skills in order to compete globally, achieve economic sustainability, and not be left behind (Ammanath, 2023; Heikkilä, 2023; UNESCO, 2022; Voss, 2022; WEF, 2022).

Additionally, AI Literacy is already an extremely important capability that all people must have in general to be effective and fully aware members of a modern civil society. Students specifically must now gain the new imperative skill of being able to effectively work with AI. Effectively being able to work with AI encompasses much more than just knowing about AI and what questions to ask. There are different specific issues associated with AI and properly using it that all must master. Teachers, students, librarians, employees, employers, everyone must develop fundamental AI Literacy in order to use AI to its fullest. But in order to fully understand all of this, we need to fully define AI Literacy.

Defining AI Literacy

Although generally considered part of Digital Literacy or Algorithmic Literacy in general (Julie et al., 2020; Ridley & Pawlick-Potts, 2021; Tinmaz et al., 2022; Yang, 2022), AI Literacy has now become of central importance yet does not have a fully agreed upon definition. To effectively address the vital issue of AI Literacy, an operational definition is needed. Professor Duri Long, a human-centered AI researcher and Brian Magerko, professor and director of graduate studies in digital media, both from Georgia Institute of Technology, provide the best overall definition of AI Literacy that I have been able to find: "a set of competencies that enables individuals to critically evaluate AI technologies; communicate and collaborate effectively with AI; and use AI as a tool online, at home, and in the workplace" (Long & Magerko, 2020, p. 2).

It is important to know that these "competencies" need to actually be more than just skills, it needs to be more of a sociocultural proactive practice that we actively pursue (Ridley & Pawlick-Potts, 2021). This overall definition is a useful and effective description because it is general enough to encompass the many different aspects of AI Literacy that will be addressed and is flexible enough to remain relevant and useful as AI continues to develop and expand in its capabilities.

Yet having a general definition of AI Literacy isn't enough to be fully AI Literate. For that we need to break AI Literacy into foundational components, its key parts that make it a vital skill that is needed by all.

Many researchers from around the world such as Duri Long and Brian Magerko from the Georgia Institute of Technology (2020), Bingcheng Wang , Pei-Luen Patrick Rau, and Tianyi Yuan from Tsinghua University, Beijing, China (2022), Siu-Cheung Kong and Guo Zhang from the National Taiwan Normal University, Taiwan (2023), and Matthias Carl Laupichler, Alexandra Aster, Tobias Raupach from Institute of Medical Education, University Hospital Bonn, Germany (2023) have put forth excellent breakdowns of key concepts or substructures of AI Literacy.

I have taken different aspects of their research and breakdowns as well as my own educational experiences, observations, and interactions with other educational professionals in the development of the following 4 key components of AI Literacy:

1. **Awareness**
2. **Capability**
3. **Knowledge**
4. **Critical Thinking**

The following chapters will present each one of these key and vital AI Literacy components, providing full definitions, explanations, examples, and detailed information on how this understanding/skill can be taught to students to prepare them for successful employment, proper civil engagement, and informed life interaction in a world filled with AI.

Component 1: Awareness

The first key component of AI Literacy is that of *Awareness*: *an awareness that AI is already all around us and is impacting society* as it continues to become integrated into more and more computer programs, apps, and processes. This idea correlates with findings by Kong et al. (2023) and researchers from the Technical University of Darmstadt, Germany, Marc Pinski and Alexander Benlian (2023). This is a key initial component of AI Literacy in that without this awareness most people will not realize the full impact of their interactions, processes, or how they might be being influenced by AI. Yet how exactly is AI all around us and how is it impacting society?

> ***"From Siri and Alexa to self-driving cars and ChatGPT, AI is transforming our world in ways that were once only imagined in science fiction"***
> (Khalatian, 2023, para. 1) – as expressed by Forbes.

A common experience for many on the internet would be to go to Gmail to check and write email, search for something on Google, write a document in Microsoft Office and then check it via Grammarly, read some news on a news site or blog, search then order something on Amazon or Alibaba, talk about it via Facebook or other social media, and then watch a movie on a streaming service like Netflix. Each one of the apps and websites listed, heavily use AI in organizing its information, tracking your interactions, possibly even creating some content, and then in giving you results/information (Adams & Chuah, 2022; Marr, 2019; Steck et al., 2021).

In some ways this is great in that by tracking everything you do and say through the programs, the AI systems get to know you and your preferences so that it can give you personalized results and information. Yet this can create a silo-ed (echo-chamber) existence in that you will start to only be exposed to your preferences and will be limited in your exposure to other possibilities/ideas.

AI in Business

Yet AI utilization goes beyond these apps and now includes additional realms and venues. Employment interviewing apps such as Hirevue use AI to help automate the assessment of written applications and video interactions to rate potential employees (Hirevue, 2023). This in itself could pose problems with who gets hired based on how the AI was trained to rank/score such evaluations as well as how information from such evaluations is further stored and used. In fact, there have been multiple legal actions to help address these complicated issues in job hiring through the use of AI (Willner, 2022).

Ken Willner, partner in the Paul Hastings Employment Law Department, states in an article on this subject "Employers are well advised to seek professional guidance with respect to the validation of AI-based and other selection tools... be mindful of the risks involved with AI assessment technology... mindful of the data collected by the AI assessment technology and ensure they comply with laws regulating the collection, use, and storage" (2022, para. 19).

AI has also become a new staple for many businesses' customer support process and chatbots, as expressed in a recent Forbes article "...generative AI is helping vendors automate quality assurance (QA) and enrich the nature of agent interactions with sophisticated insights made possible by technology like ChatGPT" (Sudhakar, 2023, para. 3).

Although AI chatbots are continually improving, there is a danger of over automation in that many people would at times, rather talk to a real person, however, as consulting data scientist Scott Robinson expresses "There's no turning back. Customer service AI is here to stay -- and it is rapidly becoming the default" (2019, para. 14).

AI in Dating and AI Companionship

AI is also being used to improve dating apps by increasing profile accuracy/reliability, enhancing long-term compatibility algorithms, and maximizing the process of people getting to know one another (Klubnikin, 2022). In an interesting survey conducted by Tidio, a chatbot development company, on 1,191 people about AI dating apps, found that a majority of people, 70%, would share private information if it meant the AI could guarantee that they would be able to meet their "dream" or "true love" partner (Szaniawska-Schiavo, 2023).

Arielle Pardes, a reporter for Wired, in talking about the use of AI in dating apps, stated "Dating apps like Tinder, Hinge, and Bumble use "collaborative filtering," which generates recommendations based on majority opinion. This is similar to the way Netflix recommends what to watch (Pardes, 2019, para. 6). Imagine the influential power that one could have on people's future relationships if these recommendations were manipulated.

Going even further, there is a growing field of study in the area of AI itself as a companion (Pfadenhauer & Lehmann, 2021). MIT researchers and other academics have found that more and more people (those with social anxiety, veterans dealing with trauma, people isolated [such as with COVID], the elderly, and many others, even those already in a relationship) are starting to use AI as a companion in different ways such as a friend or even romantic partner to help address the issue of loneliness and/or unmet needs (Alessa & Al-Khalifa, 2023; Kiron & Unruh, 2019; Le, 2023). Researchers from Baylor University and the French TBS Business School, in identifying mental health aspects of human and AI interaction, found that:

In a human-AI relationship, however, the social interaction takes place differently. AI is designed to learn its human counterpart and respond without judgment. Human users express more self-disclosures and share more personal information than their AI companions. When AI's responses are perceived to be humanlike and empathetic, a sense of friendship is formed. These same AI technologies are also being applied to the medical field. (Sullivan et al., 2023. p. 4450)

An interesting example and implementation of this comes from a news report titled *A 23-year-old Snapchat influencer used OpenAI's technology to create an A.I. version of herself that will be your girlfriend for $1 per minute* (Sternlicht, 2023). "CarynAI, is a voice-based chatbot that bills itself as a virtual girlfriend, with a voice and personality close enough to that of human Marjorie that people are willing to pay $1 per minute for a relationship with the bot...is the latest example of the stunning advances in A.I. technology that has wowed, and worried, the world over the past few months" (para. 3).

Caryn Marjorie (the real person the AI is based on), expressed how her AI incarnation really addresses the many needs of her audience (which is 99% male), "Whether you need somebody to be comforting or loving, or you just want to rant about something that happened at school or at work, CarynAI will always be there for you... You can have limitless possible reactions with CarynAI" (para. 5).

This deeply personal aspect of how AI is affecting society is nicely expressed by MIT researchers David Kiron and Gregory Unruh, "Businesses that make and sell products that replicate human connection are serving a deep need, but they may also be changing social norms in ways that can't be reversed" (2019, p. 1).

AI in Healthcare

Karen Weintraub, USA Today news reporter, in a story titled *ChatGPT is poised to upend medical information, for better and worse*, predicts that "For clinicians, these chatbots might provide a brainstorming tool, guard against mistakes and relieve some of the burden of filling out paperwork, which could alleviate burnout and allow more facetime with patients" (2023, para. 3).

Additionally, Sarah Moore from News-Medical Life Sciences, stated that "ChatGPT can assist with clinical decision support by providing real-time, evidence-based recommendations such as flagging potential drug interactions, suggesting treatment options for a specific condition, and providing relevant clinical guidelines" (2023, para. 9).

A recent study by radiologist and Georgia Institute of Technology researcher, Zeyu Zhou (2023), concluded that:

> Above all, ChatGPT has shown its potential to assist healthcare professionals in medical report writing. By leveraging this state-of-the-art language model, healthcare providers can optimize their time and resources, allowing them to focus on critical aspects of patient care. As ChatGPT continues to evolve and improve, its applications in the healthcare sector are expected to expand, ultimately contributing to more efficient and patient-centered care delivery. (para. 39)

Additionally, studies conducted by both OpenAI and academic researchers have found that ChatGPT-plus (using GPT4) is able to pass multiple medical exams due to its high amount of medical knowledge from its vast data sources (Kasai et al., 2023; OpenAI, 2023b). AI researchers from Microsoft and OpenAI, in testing ChatGPT on multiple medical exams, noted that the exceptional performance of the AI "...serves as an indicator of its potential for being harnessed in medical education and for aiding healthcare professionals with numerous aspects of healthcare delivery" (Nori et al., 2023, p. 21).

Multiple sources express that ChatGPT and similar AIs are already being used to actively help medical personnel (including physical and mental health) in evaluation and diagnosis (Doshi & Bajaj, 2023; Frąckiewicz, 2023; Jeffay, 2023). An interesting study conducted by researchers at Johns Hopkins University and the University of California went even further and reviewed the "bedside manner" or empathetic aspect of AI regarding medical interactions and found that "evaluators preferred chatbot-generated [ChatGPT] responses over physician responses 4 to 1. Additionally, chatbot responses were rated significantly higher for both quality and empathy, even when compared with the longest physician-authored responses" (2023, para. 25).

AI in Government

Governments (both national and local) have started to use AI like ChatGPT in many different ways. News agencies such as CNN, Bloomberg, Federal Times, and Semafor, have reported that governments in countries such as Japan, Costa Rica, Romania, Portugal, and the United States are now using AIs to assist with everything from advising, reporting, answering public questions, processing, and helping with administrative tasks (Badeau, 2023; Capelouto & Mendoza, 2023; Negishi, 2023; Yeung & Maruyama, 2023).

Mckinsey and Company (a highly recognized global management research and consulting firm) suggests that,

> Governments can potentially pave the way for capturing the full value of AI by... educating the private sector about the potential of AI, identifying where the biggest opportunities lie, and supporting the adoption of AI technologies in an ethical and secure manner that addresses the risks of these technologies. (Berglind, Fadia, & Isherwood, 2022)

AI has provided and will continue to provide many benefits, yet all must be aware that, as Coupler.io data analytics representative and search engine optimization specialist, Dmytro Zaichenko states,

Humans are increasingly trusting decisions made by machines. While AI adds to information clarity and data-driven decision-making, it simultaneously leads to the sameness of solutions, auto adjustments, and identical decision-making patterns. By this, I mean AI isn't capable of thinking outside of the box, acting ethically, or providing unique action points for separate cases. (2023, para. 58)

All of us, especially students, need to be mindful and fully aware that AI is now an embedded part of virtually all aspects of our environment. It has become integrated throughout and for better or worse is affecting society globally. Many researchers agree that people need to have this realization/awareness due to the importance AI is having and will continue to have on society (Farina et al., 2022). This is also highlighted in a research article by Professor and Director Spyros Makridakis of the Institute for the Future (IFF), University of Nicosia, Cyprus, regarding the most imperative challenges facing society is "utilizing the benefits of availing AI technologies, providing vast opportunities for both new products/services and immense productivity improvements while avoiding the dangers and disadvantages in terms of increased unemployment and greater wealth inequalities" (2017, p. 46).

Given the importance of this AI Literacy concept, we as teachers, professors, general instructors, and librarians must be able to fully understand this ourselves and be able to properly teach it to our students.

How to Teach the AI Literacy Concept of Awareness:

This following section presents several ways that the AI Literacy concept of Awareness can be taught to students. This can either be taught directly or integrated with other aspects of the course, or, if students have already had specific instruction on AI Literacy, it can be provided as an additional resource or scaffolding tool. Note the importance for everyone to continually develop AI Literacy skills and to develop an emotional connection with the topic in order to maximize deep learning and retention.

Discussion

This is an easy way to start to introduce each concept of AI Literacy to your students. By having an open discussion (appropriate for the class level) both the instructor and the students can identify ways that AI has become part of everyday life and the impact it is having on them (both positive and negative). Some questions that can help guide the discussion and build AI awareness include:

"What are some AI tools or processes that you or your family use every day?"

> Possible Answers: Google search (in deciding what results to show), using Siri/Alexa (in being able to understand and respond), Social Media (in choosing what engaging content to show), Online Shopping and Video Watching (in creating recommendations), etc.

"How does AI affect you and/or your family and is that good or bad or both?"

"How do you think someone could be affected by AI without them even being aware of it?"

"Why is it important that we are aware of how society is using AI and its effects?"

Simulation

This is an effective technique that can be used with each concept of AI Literacy. The following simulation prompt can be used to directly help students learn about the Awareness concept of AI Literacy. This can be assigned for students to do on their own or could be used in class with small groups or even with the entire class. Note that the following prompt can be modified but come back to this original prompt if your modifications cause issues.

An important part of giving questions to an AI system like ChatGPT are the specific words used and the way that the prompt is put together (prompt engineering). I have personally developed and tested the following prompt (on ChatGPT) and it has been shown to work and be effective in helping people learn about the important AI Literacy component of *Awareness*:

> **PROMPT:** You are a simulation machine. Your task is to present a scenario to help users understand the importance of awareness of Artificial Intelligence (AI) and how it can impact their lives. After stating the scenario, you will ask a question with multiple-choice answers for the user to choose from. Stop. Do not continue until the user has made a selection. Do not answer for the user. Please refrain from stating the consequences of each response. Instead, provide information on the potential impact of the user's chosen response. Finally, ask another question related to the scenario to further explore the topic of AI awareness. Encourage users to consider the potential outcomes of their choices in the scenario.

Role-Play

This is another great way that an instructor can help students understand this AI Literacy concept of Awareness. Here are some ideas:

Scenario One: Social Media User

One student plays the role of an avid social media user who spends several hours a day on various platforms. The student notices that their social media feeds are filled with posts and advertisements that align with their political views, and rarely come across opposing viewpoints. The student is concerned about the potential bias in AI algorithms and wants to discuss it with another student, a friend.

Scenario Two: Autonomous Vehicle

Three to five students are passengers in an autonomous vehicle. As they are riding to their destination they discuss the benefits of AI in taking over the driving of vehicles (such as reducing accidents and improving transportation efficiency). They also discuss some ethical dilemmas and safety concerns pertaining to AI decision-making in complex driving situations.

Scenario Three: Newspaper AI

Four students have just heard that their favorite major newspaper will be reducing its staff of news reporters by 75%. It will instead use AI to generate news based on other news feeds and social media. Students discuss ethical issues and societal impacts of such a move by a major newspaper.

Awareness that AI is already all around us and is impacting society is just one needed aspect of AI Literacy. Awareness is not enough to fully grasp the overall skills needed to properly use AI. Another very important concept is that of *Capability* in effectively using AI.

Component 2: Capability

The second key component of AI Literacy is that of *Capability: knowing how to use AI properly and confidently when needed*. This involves being capable of choosing the right AI for the job/project as well as being able to interact with the AI as effectively as possible (known as *prompt engineering*).

This specifically empowers an individual's affective dimension in gaining "new abilities and ways to participate in digital society" (Kong & Zhang, 2021, p. 13). Additionally, this AI Literacy capability will enable individuals to creatively apply knowledge learned to new contexts/situations and leverage these benefits to better contribute to society (Kong et al., 2023).

Part of having capability with AI is in knowing that there are a lot of different types of AI. There are highly complex back-end AIs that do lots of different types of data mining and advanced processes, as well as direct access type AIs such as ChatGPT large language models that let you interact with it directly. Although this book focuses on ChatGPT, there are other LLM competitors such as Google's Bard and Microsoft's Bing Chat (which also uses OpenAI's GPT4).

There are also powerful and publically accessible math AIs such as WolfgramAlpha (https://www.wolframalpha.com), text-to-image AIs such as MidJounrey (https://www.midjourney.com), Stable Diffusion (https://stability.ai), and Dall-E 2 (https://openai.com/product/dall-e-2), and even text-to-video AIs such as Runway Gen-2 (https://research.runwayml.com/gen2) – other text-to-video tools have been reported but are not yet available from Meta, Google (Dreamix), and more (Molad et al, 2023; Wolfe, 2023). Additionally, through the use of APIs, many companies exist and will continue to become available that offer specific uses or personalized interfaces to pre-existing AI's such as SnapChat, SalesForce, Instacart, Shopify, Ambience Health, Khan Academy, and more (Heikkilä, 2023b; Khan, 2023; Tellez, 2023).

Future implementations (as already hinted in GPT4) will be able to combine the abilities of multiple AIs to allow for multiple capabilities (such as those listed) through a single interface. This is another reason why we must continue to be aware of ongoing developments in the capabilities of AI, to better harness its power. Along with these different types of AIs we need to know what AIs can do.

Many of the AIs previously listed are self-explanatory regarding what they do (create images, videos, solve math equations, etc.), but ChatGPT is somewhat different. Although many in academia still only see ChatGPT and similar AI as cheating machines (AP, 2023), this type of AI is capable of so much more.

The only real utilization limitations are in the creativity of its users. ChatGPT has been used successfully to: write poems, songs, stories, scripts, essays, computer code (as well as debugging), emails, descriptions for products, and even prompts for other AIs like image creation AI, Midjourney.

Specifically, in academia, ChatGPT is used for helping instructors write syllabi, welcome letters, policies, student learning objectives, rubrics, course outlines, learning activities, assignments / assessments, scaffolding components, and much more (see the *Bonus Section: Prompt Examples & Resources* chapter of this book, my other book "ChatGPT AI in Education: What it is and How to Use it in the Classroom," and my YouTube site for more information and examples).

ChatGPT can also be directly used by students to: explain concepts, summarize information, explain/summarize at different levels of sophistication (example prompt: "explain the concept of quantum dynamics as if I am in 5th grade"), act as a study buddy (create quizzes, flashcards, foreign language conversation, ask questions in different ways and provide different types of feedback), act as a simulation, game, and much more.

Both the instructor and the student become more empowered when increasing their AI capability which can then also be used to better personalize the learning experience.

Prompt Engineering

The other aspect of capability is that of being able to properly ask questions or *prompt* the AI. This is important to get the best responses from the AI by being effective with time and limiting frustration. Although these AIs allow for simple interaction via conversational English, the better the prompts are created, the better the overall result. In fact, this has become a major subskill within AI Literacy as eloquently expressed by professional AI university educator/consultant, author, artist, and general AI evangelist Kris Kashtanova,

> In my eight months of doing A.I. full-time as a job, I rarely used my Computer Science degree and used prompting skills a lot. It's not even about learning how to prompt a particular platform but learning fast how each platform is prompted and adapting to change to get what your client wants... some say that prompt writing will be replaced by more intuitive systems. Yes, but we live here and now. In the job market right now prompt writing is something companies pay for, when and if it is replaced you'll learn the new way and adapt. (Kashtanova, 2023)

A similar sentiment was expressed by reporter Nik Popli, in a recent article for Times magazine talking about the high demand from prompt engineers, when quoting Andrej Karpathy, former chief of AI for Tesla, who stated that "The hottest new programming language is English" (2023, para. 15).

Students need to know that prompt engineering skills are extremely important, and yet we in academia need to fully understand what the subskills are in its development. Important subskills to develop in being a better prompt engineer are: grammar/vocabulary, logic, patience/persistence, analytical skills, problem-solving skills, attention to detail, creative thinking, critical thinking, formulation, and some basic understanding of AI (machine learning and large language models) and its limitations (data sources, ability to understand, accuracy, memory limits). Additionally, the more that someone knows about a particular field, the better they will be able to know the type of questions to ask and how different concepts go together in order to create the best prompt, yielding the best results.

Some general principles of good prompt engineering are:
- Be specific to ensure that the AI fully understands what you are talking about. You may need to give a specific purpose to better explain or even an example of what you are wanting. Giving the system more context will also help.

- Avoid ambiguous words, terms, or pronouns – *would you be able to understand it?*

- Be concise to help keep the AI on task and provide the most useful output.

- Word order can be very important. Think about how a person might not understand what you really meant to say if your words or sentences are slightly out of order, it could cause the AI to interpret what you meant in a totally different way.

- Ask for a specific level of complexity: "Please write a *university-level* essay on____"

- Have the AI assume the perspective (persona) of a specific career field or person: "Assume the role of a university professor in the field of ____ in describing ____."

- If a prompt isn't giving you the results you want, try changing some of the words, its order, and/or its sentence structure, as well as even adding the word "please." At times, an AI system like ChatGPT can understand better if a prompt is made more conversational.

Additionally, review some of the different ChatGPT prompt examples that are provided throughout this book.

Co-writing is also a related skill in that although it does use prompt engineering, it also requires more. In Co-writing, a student/writer will need to be able *to write with* the AI which is very different from just having the AI *write for* the student/writer.

To begin with, one would need to have an understanding that prompting the AI to create an initial text would just be the beginning. From there, it would require a proper review of the text and either a fine-tuning of the initial prompt or editing of the resulting text. The writer in this process would need to use many skills to check for logic, correctness, flow, and different aspects (such as it meeting all rubric requirements in the case of a student) to ensure that results are of the highest quality.

*Academia needs to seriously consider what skills are being focused on and developed to help students gain the abilities needed to continually stay relevant, be able to properly function in a rapidly developing world, and best compete on a global scale. This then needs to affect the university, degree, general education student learning objectives/outcomes in order to be properly nested and fully addressed within a student's educational experience.

Yet any and all skills should be constantly evaluated and updated since AI like ChatGPT and others are continually being updated and improved upon. Although prompt engineering is in high demand now due to the nature of the AI systems, perhaps future systems will not need that type of skill and other focuses such as specialized types of creativity and emotional development will be needed. This area needs to be continually monitored by academia, with systems, administrators, and instructors needing to be flexible and able to continually adapt to stay relevant and useful.

Overreliance

In addition to the importance of gaining new skills (capabilities), we must also be conscious of the possibility of losing current skills. Losing basic skills can occur when an AI system becomes very good and takes over tasks that use to be done by people. The less there is a need to check that the AI is properly doing the task, the more a person will trust the system, which will lead to overreliance. This overreliance will then become a bias, which can cause a person to give more weight (over trust = rely) to recommendations from an AI system over a human recommendation because the person using the AI system does "...not have enough knowledge and skills to properly evaluate AI recommendations" as explained by AI researchers from Microsoft Samir Passi and Mihaela Vorvoreanu (2022, p. 6).

OpenAI, the company that created ChatGPT, has even warned about the issue of overreliance in a recent technical paper on the GPT4 language which is the newer language currently being used by ChatGPT Plus,

Overreliance occurs when users excessively trust and depend on the model, potentially leading to unnoticed mistakes and inadequate oversight. This can happen in various ways: users may not be vigilant for errors due to trust in the model; they may fail to provide appropriate oversight based on the use case and context; or they may utilize the model in domains where they lack expertise, making it difficult to identify mistakes... dependency on the model may hinder the development of new skills or even lead to the loss of important skills. Overreliance is a failure mode that likely increases with model capability and reach. (OpenAI, 2023b, p. 59)

This aspect of AI overreliance is also well expressed by author, college writing teacher, and critical AI literacy advocate Anna Mills, in an article by The Register news publication,

It's too tempting to use it [AI] as a crutch, skip the thinking, and skip the frustrating moments of writing. Some of that is part of the process of going deeper and wrestling with ideas. There is a risk of learning loss if students become dependent and don't develop the writing skills they need. (Quach, 2022, para. 26)

So how do we prevent overreliance and ensure that skills are not lost? As OpenAI advises in its technical paper, "mitigating overreliance requires multiple defenses" (2023b, p. 60). First, we need to be realistic and honest regarding the skills that might be lost. Are they fundamental, basic skills mastery, type skills that all students should have in order to fully understand processes and concepts at a higher level, or, are they skills that although valued, are no longer fully necessary since a fully reliable system can now accommodate in a much better way? This is a complex concept that all of us in academia really need to think about.

Although comparing AI like ChatGPT to a calculator is a bit overdone, it provides a good comparison. We still want all students to have basic understanding of numbers and mathematical processes, but we no longer require them to be able to do long computations in their head. A student can now accomplish much more by working *with* the technology, in this case, the calculator. In a similar manner, for many years, the physical act of writing, meaning having good penmanship, was a very important skill that students spent many hours developing. Now, thanks to technology, it is considered a lost art that although valued, isn't *needed* as it once was.

Another important way to help minimize overreliance on AI is through human oversight in multiple ways. One way is by ensuring that students and all users of AI have full access to and an understanding of the AI systems' actual capabilities and limitations; what it can actually do and that no system is perfect (OpenAI, 2023; Passi & Vorvoreanu, 2022; Verdicchio & Perin, 2022).

Other aspects of human oversight in mitigating overreliance on AI would be for an AI system to provide a confidence score on the information provided or for a system to express that a user is going to accept an AI recommendation with a low recommendation score (Passi & Vorvoreanu, 2022). These are implementation ideas that could be integrated into future ChatGPT implementations and are currently addressed via warnings on some information (results) provided by the AI system.

OpenAI's ChatGPT technical paper, in its section on mitigation of AI overreliance, additionally recommends

> ...to generally avoid misleading claims or implications—including that it is human—and to consider the potential impact of changes to the model's style, tone, or perceived personality on users. We also suggest that developers communicate to users the importance of critically evaluating model outputs. (2023, p. 60)

This is to help address the psychological aspect of many people wanting to trust an authoritative computer, especially if it is able to give calculations and recommendations in mere seconds (Bogert et al., 2021; Passi & Vorvoreanu, 2022; Verdicchio & Perin, 2022).

A final and important way to help address overreliance on AI is through the teaching of AI Literacy skills. Multiple academics and AI researchers have expressed that reminding users of the information presented in this book and directly teaching AI Literacy skills will better help students develop the necessary skills to be able to use AI properly as a tool without overly relying on the system (Dai et al., 2023; Dwivedi et al, 2023; Passi & Vorvoreanu, 2022; Sallam et al, 2023; Strauß, 2021). This is yet another reason why everyone in academia must have valid AI Literacy sources and integrate this teaching into all levels of education.

Academic Dishonesty

An associated derivation that can manifest from overreliance is that of cheating (academic dishonesty) by using an AI system like ChatGPT to complete assignments/assessments such as an essay when not allowed. In this case, a student would be over-reliant on AI to the point of wanting/needing it to complete the student's work even to the detriment of the student's learning process. To help address this issue of overreliance (cheating by using AI inappropriately) the following is recommended:

- **Ensure that there is no ambiguity regarding what is allowed and what isn't, when AI can be used, when it can't, and what constitutes academic integrity misconduct.** Educational institutions need to ensure that their policies and procedures are clear, fully accessible to students, continuously expressed to the student (posters, presentations, events, competitions, etc.), and that consequences/ramifications are known to students, ensuring that they know that violators are caught and rules are properly and fairly enforced. This is important so that there is a culture of high value in upholding academic integrity.

- **Faculty need to additionally ensure that students are aware of when the use of AI is allowed.** This should be done through discussion in the classroom and including specific information in the syllabus, assignment instructions, and even assessment rubrics.

- **Use both formative and summative assessments.** Help the student develop the necessary knowledge/skills to be able to do the overall assignment by doing subtasks, developmental assignments, with appropriate feedback. In the case of writing assignments, the seven-step writing process could be utilized with students having to turn in something for each part of the process. This also helps keep the student accountable for their learning and lowers the use of an AI system. The following infographics highlights this process and allows for the instructor to decide where integration and utilization of AI could be implemented:

Ways to Integrate ChatGPT in the Writing Process OR Ways to Make Writing Assignments More Resistant

By Brent A. Anders from the book: *ChatGPT AI in Education*

Ways to INTEGRATE/USE ChatGPT	7-Step Writing Process	Ways to Make Assignments More RESISTANT to ChatGPT
1. ChatGPT to research potential topics and present options	1. **CHOOSING A TOPIC:** Contemplate, research, & reflect, then decide on the appropriate essay topic.	1. Done in class, use specific sources
2. ChatGPT to help brainstorm ideas around a specific subject/idea	2. **BRAINSTORMING:** Come up with as many good & bad ideas as you can. Review and select the best one.	2. Done in class, require a mind map / visual representation
3. ChatGPT to create an outline *Students verify the logic	3. **OUTLINING:** Structure essay into levels within the intro, body (supporting main idea), & conclusion.	3. Done in class, require specific-personal reasons, class discussion, answer why
4. ChatGPT creates *Students use critical thinking, checks for coherence, and adds personalization	4. **DRAFTING:** Complete (full sentences, almost perfect) manuscript ready to be reviewed.	4. Highly local/post 2021 content, include class discussion (answer why), annotated bibliography
5. ChatGPT gives feedback *Students verify, thoroughly checking citations/references	5. **SOLICITING FEEDBACK:** Have someone review your draft and offer suggestions (review rubric)	5. Conduct in-class Peer Evaluations
6. ChatGPT implements feedback *Students would verify logic	6. **REVISING:** Address/fix all feedback issues and continue to strengthen/clarify the essay	6. Discuss in class, require annotated bibliography, answer why changes were made from draft
7. ChatGPT used to review *Student submits final version	7. **PROOFREADING:** Final review, ensure all is perfect	7. ChatGPT used to review *Student submits final product

Sovorel Educational Blog: sovorelpublishing.com

- **An additional low-stakes (point) assessment such as a quiz could be done (even in writing classes) to help ensure students know the content without AI assistance.** Periodic, short, in-class quizzes (short answer/multiple choice) could be used to help ensure that students are held accountable for their learning and can express their capabilities without AI assistance when needed.

- **Use more dynamic assessments.** The utilization and inclusion of more dynamic assessments such as Project Based Learning assignments, class presentations, or creation projects such as student videos, podcasts, posters, etc., would be another method of assessment that would help to require students demonstrate their skills and capability, beyond just a finished written product.

- **Faculty must ensure students fully know the relevancy of why they are learning the topic AND why they are not allowed to use AI to do the assignment/assessment.** Motivation needs to be maximized by fully explaining the need to learn the basic aspects (basic skills mastery) before using/working with the AI on other assignments or in subsequent classes.

- **Use AI such as ChatGPT to create needed scaffolding and study aids to help students prepare.** Through ChatGPT AI, more support can be offered to students to help them understand, learn, and have confidence in success thereby leading to less reliance on inappropriate use of AI = fewer incidents of academic dishonesty. Use ChatGPT to create alternative summaries at different levels of complexity, additional quizzes, games, simulations, topic stories, analogies, examples, etc. to scaffold learning and help students fully prepare for assessments (see *Bonus Section: Prompt Examples & Resources*).

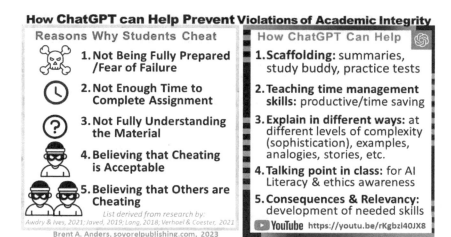

How ChatGPT can Help Prevent Violations of Academic Integrity

Reasons Why Students Cheat	How ChatGPT Can Help
1. Not Being Fully Prepared /Fear of Failure	1. **Scaffolding:** summaries, study buddy, practice tests
2. Not Enough Time to Complete Assignment	2. **Teaching time management skills:** productive/time saving
3. Not Fully Understanding the Material	3. **Explain in different ways:** at different levels of complexity (sophistication), examples, analogies, stories, etc.
4. Believing that Cheating is Acceptable	4. **Talking point in class:** for AI Literacy & ethics awareness
5. Believing that Others are Cheating	5. **Consequences & Relevancy:** development of needed skills

List derived from research by: Awdry & Ives, 2021; Javed, 2019; Lang, 2018; Verhoel & Coester, 2021

YouTube https://youtu.be/rKgbzI40JX8

Brent A. Anders, sovorelpublishing.com, 2023

- **Careful use of AI Text and Plagiarism software.** Letting students know that AI Text and Plagiarism software exists (such as new features built into Turnitin [Turnitin, 2023]) can help motivate some students to do the right thing, but be aware that there are no detection systems that are 100% reliable, they can be easily circumvented, and some systems can create different levels of false-positives (saying text is AI generated or plagiarized when it isn't), (Krishna et al., 2023; Sovorel, 2023). Work to better know your students' writing for comparison as well as implement the other suggestions expressed to help mitigate the issue.

Writing Assignments in the Age of AI

Instructional techniques, activities to consider:

Use some or all of these ideas to help ensure students are approriately doing the work required.

Allowable AI Usage

- Clearly stated on Syllabus
- Clearly defined in Rubrics
- Reiterated in Assignment Instructions
- Remind students about Academic Integrity
- AI Literacy incorporated into courses
- Explicit clear relevancy given to students as to why or why not regarding use of AI for an assignment/eval

★ Break up the writing assignments into different parts (such as the 7-step writing process: topic, brainstorming, outline, rough draft, etc.)
  - some parts could be done in class
  - some parts could use AI, *if allowed*

★ Require an annotated bibliography (make students explain why they specifically chose their references)

★ Require a rough draft done with "track changes" on to see their work/development

★ Class discussion about topics chosen: the student should be fully involved in the process and able to explain why they are writing about different topic aspects

★ Incorporate a graded oral presentation: this would help ensure that the student learned about the topic and can answer on the spot questions about it

★ Increase penalties for false or made-up "hallucinated" in-text citations, references, and quotes - helps ensure more time spent proofreading, knowing text

★ Clearly explain the skills being developed in going through the writing process, & not using AI at this time on this assignment

★ Consider when to develop using AI for written assignments skills

Created by Brent A. Anders, Sovorel: www.sovorelpublishing.com

These suggestions correlate with findings and recommendations from research conducted by SCION Research Group, DREC – Plymouth Marjon University, Plymouth, UK; PAC - School of Biological and Marine Sciences, University of Plymouth, Plymouth, UK, (Cotton, Cotton, & Shipway, 2023).

Understanding Limitations

Along with gaining capabilities with AI and as a noted way to help address overreliance, we must also fully understand the limitations of AI. AI capabilities are continually growing, however many of those additional capabilities or utilizations require the use of APIs or third-party systems that are not part of regular/free ChatGPT. That is important to realize in order to use the right AI system for a given task. Whereas some AI systems such as the new ChatGPT Plus, Microsoft Chat, and Google Bard can use the current Internet to find up-to-date information, the current free version of regular ChatGPT is limited to information mainly up to 2021. Although aspects such as these might change in the near future, it is important to know the limitations and capabilities of any AI system that is being used.

Hallucinations:

AI systems are also not perfect and can sometimes give false information. This information is sometimes presented in a way that seems confidently correct but is actually inaccurate or completely made up and is often referred to as a "hallucination" in science research (OpenAI, 2023b). Yet due to the nature of the technology, it is continually improving with the AI system, being able to become more and more accurate:

> GPT-4 significantly reduces hallucinations relative to previous GPT-3.5 models (which have themselves been improving with continued iteration). GPT-4 scores 19 percentage points higher than our latest GPT-3.5 on our internal, adversarially-designed factuality evaluations (Figure 6). (OpenAI, 2023b, p. 10)

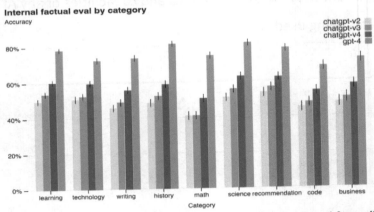

Figure 6. Performance of GPT-4 on nine internal adversarially-designed factuality evaluations. Accuracy is shown on the y-axis, higher is better. An accuracy of 1.0 means the model's answers are judged to be in agreement with human ideal responses for all questions in the eval. (OpenAI, 2023b, p. 10)

Sentience/Consciousness:

Another important limitation that many people find difficult to understand, given the high capabilities of these AI systems, is that these AI systems are not sentient or have a human-like consciousness in any way – as expressed by cognitive psychologist, author, and philosopher David Chalmers while presenting at a Neural Information Processing Systems conference (2023). Additionally, the head of R&D and Ethics Consultant for BABL AI and Associate Professor of Philosophy at the University of Iowa, Ali Hasan explained that,

> ...it is hard to resist believing, explicitly or implicitly, that chatGPT works via some non-human, non-conscious states and processes that are a kind of quasi-understanding, something that functions much like understanding, or that tracks what we understand... But in fact, we don't have a good reason to think that LLMs have this kind of quasi-understanding, or a model of the world that ordinary language is about. To think that it does is to anthropomorphize chatGPT by proxy. (Hasan, 2023, p.9)

AI systems like ChatGPT do not really understand (in the same way that a human does) what they are saying in that they are using a predictive algorithm (along with some other "temperature" parameters) to come up with the best usable solution/output (Feingold, 2023; OpenAI, 2023b).

Although some researchers and academics predict that the development of sentient AI will happen at some point (possibly soon), there are huge variances as to when that will happen (Gordon, 2022; Ray, 2022; Valero de Urquia 2023).

Another limitation that also ties into ethical aspects deals with how the AI system actually works. The theoretical aspects of AIs are known; it uses a neural network, machine learning, LLMs, and large scale predictive analysis with temperature manipulation in its responses, but exact specifics aren't fully articulated by these private companies leaving it to be a bit of a black-box.

OpenAI's own technical paper expresses duality in this limitation by stating "Given both the competitive landscape and the safety implications of large-scale models like GPT-4, this report contains no further details about the architecture (including model size), hardware, training compute, dataset construction, training method, or similar" (OpenAI, 2023b, p. 2). Yet then later states "...we especially encourage more research into: Interpretability, explainability, and calibration, to address the current nature of "black-box" AI models. We also encourage research into effective means of promoting AI literacy to aid appropriate scrutiny to model outputs" (p. 69).

How to Teach the AI Literacy Concept of Capability:

Discussion

This instructional can always be used and is a low-stakes way to at least talk about this concept of AI Literacy and help students understand this concept of Capability. Some good varied questions on this concept would include:

- What types of AIs are there?
- Why are there different types of AIs?

- How can students use ChatGPT and similar LLMs to help in their learning process?
- What is *overreliance on AI* and why is that a bad thing?
- How can overreliance on AI lead to academic integrity misconduct?
- What can we do to help prevent inappropriate overreliance on AI?
- What are some AI limitations?
- What does "hallucination" mean regarding AI?
- Is AI alive?

Discussion is always good, but to gain true *capability*, students need to use the system in some way.

Simulation

This is a great way to help students learn by going through a simulated scenario and having to interact with an AI and make a choice. The following simulation will help students, either individually, in pairs, as small groups, or even as a class, help to identify better prompts for different situations:

PROMPT: You are a simulation machine. Your task is to present a scenario to help users understand the importance of properly developing a good prompt when asking Artificial Intelligence (AI) like ChatGPT a question. Please do not give away the solution in your scenario. After stating the scenario, you will ask the user to select the best prompt with multiple-choice answers for the user to choose from. Stop. Do not answer for the user. Do not continue until the user has made a selection. After the user has given a response, please give feedback on the user's selection. Finally, ask another question related to the scenario to further develop the user's ability to identify the best prompt.

The following simulation is a bit more advanced in that students are not selecting from different choices and are instead asked to create their own prompt for the given problem scenario. The AI system would then provide feedback based on their response. Students could be asked to provide screen captures, video captures, or photos of the interaction with the AI to help prove that they went through it for assignment/assessment/participation purposes.

PROMPT: You are a simulation machine. Your task is to present a scenario to help users understand the importance of properly developing a good prompt when asking Artificial Intelligence (AI) like ChatGPT a question. Please do not give away the solution in your scenario. After stating the scenario, you will ask the user to create a prompt to ask an AI like ChatGPT. Stop. Do not answer for the user. Do not continue until the user has made a selection. After the user has given a response, please give feedback on the user's selection. Finally, ask another question related to the scenario to further develop the user's ability to identify the best prompt.

Hands-on Learning

This would be the most effective means of learning for this concept in that students would be able to learn by doing. A simple idea could be a low-stakes assignment where you ask students to come up with a good prompt for a problem (such as an aspect from their major, the class, or something else – *see previous simulation for more examples*). They could then use an AI system like ChatGPT in pairs, small groups, or together with everyone if done within the class.

Alternatively, this could be done as a take-home assignment where students would go through the process of prompting ChatGPT and then further refine that prompt based on the results. Students could be asked to turn in screenshots or video captures of their interactions. – Along with this, it would be important for students to reflect on what they experienced and then discuss the situation and what was learned from it. In this way, students gain a better understanding of the awareness and capability portions of AI Literacy.

In addition to the vital aspects of both *Awareness* of AI and how it is affecting society as well as *Capability* in using AI and the associated issue of overreliance, a third key concept is that of *Knowledge* of who can use AI and how.

Component 3: Knowledge

The third component of AI Literacy is knowledge, the knowledge that anyone can now use AI to including students, instructors, businesses, their competitors, governments, people from other countries, and all other groups and agencies. This includes people who want to use AI for good, as well as those who want to use AI for negative - dishonest reasons such as scams, revenge, or simply to disrupt order or influence people disingenuously. The aspect of knowledge has been recognized as an important aspect of overall AI Literacy by many AI professionals, to include German AI researchers from the Institute of Medical Education, University Hospital Bonn, Bonn, Germany, Matthias Laupichler, Alexandra Aster, and Tobias Raupach (2023) and Bingcheng Wang, Pei-Luen Rau, and Tianyi Yuan from the Department of Industrial Engineering, Tsinghua University, Beijing, People's Republic of China (2022).

Personal Data

Part of this concept of knowledge is in understanding how one's personal information (data) is being collected and used, as well as what type of privacy and protection (security) is being provided for said data. As an example, ChatGPT states "We don't use data for selling our services, advertising, or building profiles of people—we use data to make our models more helpful for people. ChatGPT, for instance, improves by further training on the conversations people have with it" (OpenAI, 2023c, para. 9).

Thanks to a recent settlement in Italy where ChatGPT was temporarily banned because that country felt that the AI was violating certain EU privacy policies, users can now turn off chat history and prevent the system from using their data for model training, and age verification is now required in EU countries (Chan, 2023).

Another competing, public AI with similar aspects to ChatGPT states:

We collect any information that you provide to us, including when you create your account, submit your preferences, or contact us. We also collect information about your device and the ways you use and interact with our Services... We use the information we collect to understand and analyze how you use our Services and develop new products, services, features, and functionality; for marketing purposes, such as developing and providing promotional materials that may be useful, relevant, valuable or otherwise of interest to you... (You, 2023).

Everyone needs to know how an AI system is collecting and using their information. In academia, this is important to ensure that students are protected and that private information (such as in using an AI to help grade an assignment) is not exposed to an AI system that might reuse the information in an unwanted way.

AI Terms

Knowledge of AI terms is another important aspect of this component in order to have better AI Literacy. To better keep up with ongoing new developments in the field of AI, having a basic understanding of terms such as:

LLMs (large language models): used with statistical and probabilistic techniques to decide the probability of different words occurring within a sentence)

Narrow AI: AI focused on one task, *general AI* (AI that can do many tasks to due to human-like intelligence)

Machine learning: use of data and algorithms to imitate how humans learn and improve, will help when going through reading and audio/video informational resources.

*For an expanded view of *AI Terms* see the Glossary section towards the end of this book.

AI Created Content (Deepfakes & Fake News)

Everyone, especially students, needs the vital knowledge that any content: text, audio, video, other, may have been created or (deepfaked) through the use of an AI for purposes of entertainment or research, as well as for negative reasons such as to scam (cheat people out of money), to influence, for fame, revenge, or to cause fear/confusion – as identified by cognitive, linguistic, and psychological sciences researchers from Brown University (Nieweglowska et al., 2023) and Business researchers from Monash University, Malaysia (Kwok & Koh, 2021).

Recently (March/April 2023) AI created images were made of French President Emmanuel Macron and the protests occurring in France due to a controversial bill increasing the retirement age needed to get government benefits (Mouriquand, 2023; Olson, 2023). These images were posted on social media and were viewed by millions of people around the world. Many people did not initially know that these were fake images created by AI.

Due to the photo-realistic capabilities of modern AI along with the free and relatively easy access to these systems, more and more people will be creating these types of images and unleashing them to the world, which will then be shared and will most often lose its specific context, explanation, or warning statement that it is an AI created document (if it ever originally had such a statement).

Highly esteemed Computer Science professor and former Google AI researcher, Geoffrey Hinton, often referred to as the "Godfather of AI," expressed these same types of worries in an interview with the *New York Times* "… the internet will be flooded with false photos, videos and text, and the average person will not be able to know what is true anymore" (Metz, 2023, para. 21).

Photo Source: Mouriquand, 2023, Euronews article attribute image by simply referencing Midjourney and "Copyright Reddit – Twitter" – reverse image search via Google did not yield conclusive results for better attribution, but may have been made by Twitter handle "No Context French" (Olson, 2023).

Another interesting example of an AI generated image is the following fake image of Russian President Vladimir Putin kissing the hand of Chinese President Xi Jinping during the Chinese leader's recent trip to the Russian nation in March 2023 (Weber, 2023):

Photo Source: "Jason Jay Smart" as cited by Joscha Weber from DW
German news, 2023

Other examples include a fake image of an elderly man bloody from
being beaten by French police during retirement age protests (AFP
News Agency, 2023) and the Pope in a stylish puffy winter jacket
(Daley, 2023).

Photo Source for Pope in Puffy Jacket: Daley, 2023, artist: Pablo Xavier, using Midjourney AI (Cartter, 2023). Photo Source for older man beaten by police: AFB News Agency, 2023, artist: Régis Gonzalez using Midjourney AI.

The issues with these types of images are that they create a false narrative, imply false/misleading information, and induce an emotional response that could affect some people's opinion or feelings towards an individual or event. As an example, just imagine the effects that these types of images could have on elections throughout the world.

Another example is AI-developed audio/videos such as deepfakes. In 2022 a deepfake video went viral that portrayed Ukrainian President Volodymyr Zelenskyy, apparently surrendering to Russia (FRANCE 24 English, 2022).

And now I decide to say goodbye to you. I advise you to lay down your arms and return to your families.

TRUTH∎FAKE

Debunking a deepfake video of Zelensky telling Ukrainians to surrender · FRANCE 24 English
Screenshot from: https://youtu.be/2tgqX5WVhr0

This video was quickly shown to be a fake, but detecting fake videos has become extremely challenging now, as described in a news interview with Dr. Paromita Pain, an assistant professor of global media at the Reynolds School of Journalism, University of Nevada, Reno, "Detecting deepfakes is getting more difficult as the technology that creates deepfakes is getting more sophisticated... Oftentimes, the research that is designed to help detect deepfakes just ends up helping make deepfake technology better"(Britt, 2023, para. 5). Imagine the fallout, confusion, and havoc that can occur by using this technology in the wrong way.

Everyone needs to be aware of the many negative and deceptive ways that AI like this can be used. Everything from scam telephone calls that sounds just like someone you know due to AI-generated audio to phony presidential news conferences (even in real-time) are now possible.

Additionally, many in academia (New York University, NOVA School of Science and Technology, Oakland University, University of Engineering and Technology-Taxila, University of Michigan) and the media (NPR, Sky News) expect the use of deceptive deepfakes and other negative AI utilizations to greatly increase due to AIs improved ease of use, speed, and affordability to produce (Masood et al., 2023; Mehta et al., 2023; Parks & Bond, 2023, Sky News Australia, 2023).

It is important to know these aspects of AI and its abilities with images, audio, and videos in order to have fuller knowledge of AI, but it is a disservice to only focus on the negative.

Using AI to create images, audio, and videos has many positives in that it is fun and exciting (even motivational), it is a vital aspect of movie special effects, it is democratizing in many ways by empowering regular people to create high-quality art that was previously out of reach, it allows for free expression and a way to help describe feelings or ideas, and it can greatly help students and businesses via fast, high-quality, low-cost image/audio/video development.

Additionally, it can serve as a great tool in learning by serving as another educational technology for use in different ways. Imagine the creativity that can be unleashed by students as they create images, animations, and videos of their explanations of concepts, ideas, or learning experiences.

As an example, check out this video where only free AI tools are used to create all parts of a short documentary film: https://youtu.be/h3AhYJ8YVss.

To maximize our knowledge of AI, we have to realize that there is so much good that AI can be used for as well as multiple negative possibilities. Yet even with the increasing capabilities of AI in every type of medium (images, audio, video), research from multiple fields has shown that through proper education, development of AI literacy (specifically critical thinking), people can better understand AI in general and be more resistant to fake news/images or deceptive use of AI (Apuke, et al., 2022; Shin & Lee, 2022; Vargas-Bianchi et al., 2023).

How to Teach the AI Literacy Concept of Knowledge:

Discussion

This component of AI Literacy will lend itself well to discussion in that it deals with knowledge and understanding. Questions regarding what different AI terms mean, the importance of knowing what is happening with personal data, and AI-created content such as deepfakes can be subjects for a great discussion.

Quiz

A lot of the Knowledge component of AI Literacy can also be used within a quiz to help students show what they have learned. Use the following prompt as an example of how a quiz like this can be easily created through the help of AI like ChatGPT:

PROMPT: create 10 quiz questions, some multiple choice, some fill in the blank, based on the following information: LLMs: large language models (used with statistical and probabilistic techniques to decide the probability of different words occurring within a sentence), narrow AI (AI focused on one task), general AI (AI that can do many tasks to due to human-like intelligence), machine learning (use of data and algorithms to imitate how humans learn and improve) will help when going through reading and audio/video informational resources. After the questions give me an answer sheet.

Hands-on Learning

Nothing beats good student-centered hands-on learning, especially with a topic like deepfakes in AI Literacy. You could put students in groups and use Project Based Learning (PBL) to have them create a deepfake on their own. They could be free to use different types of software and AI to go through the process. Although a final product would be a component, the key would be for them to learn about the process, how easy was it, what options were available, what about the quality, is it ethical for the implementation they are using it for, what could happen if it would be used deceptively? A great component of this would be reflections that students could write up or share in their PBL presentations.

Along with the needed aspects of *Awareness* of AI and how it is affecting society, understanding and developing *Capability* in using AI along with the associated issue of overreliance, and having *Knowledge* of who can use AI, key terms, and ways it can be used (scams, deepfakes, etc.), we must also learn the vital AI Literacy component of *Critical Thinking*.

Component 4: Critical Thinking

Although all aspects of AI Literacy are important, and mastery of each concept creates an enhanced synergistic effect, the fourth component of *Critical Thinking* is perhaps the most vital aspect for all people to understand and is listed as a major part of critical thinking by many researchers (Laupichler et al., 2023; Long & Magerko, 2020; Wang et al., 2022).

Yet, although this term is used a lot in academia, business, and elsewhere, we need to have a good operational definition for the purposes of using it as a vital component of AI Literacy.

Defining Critical Thinking

John Dewey, a highly regarded 20th-century teacher, author and philosopher of education in the United States, generally referred to what we now call critical thinking as *reflective thinking* and defined it as "active, persistent and careful consideration of any belief or supposed form of knowledge in the light of the grounds that support it, and the further conclusions to which it tends... something is believed in (or disbelieved in), not on its own direct account, but through something else which stands as witness, evidence, proof, voucher, warrant" (1910, pp. 6-8).

Additionally, modern research has identified specific attributes and processes needed for effective critical thinking:

- Maintaining an attitude of critical awareness (reflective and primed, on the lookout for issues/inconsistencies)
- Interpretation (ability to develop meaning and understanding by questioning)
- Utilization of Active Listening to help ensure proper observation/receipt of the info provided
- Open Mindedness (willing to look at different perspectives, opinions, ideas)
- Skeptical of Extreme Views (realization that most things are not black or white and are usually in the grey zone: somewhere in the middle)

- Evidence Focused and Self-Regulating (actively pursuing evidence, considering of emotions within oneself and others, but not letting it overweigh facts)
- Analysis/Evaluations (looking at individual parts, and verifying credibility)
- Ability to use both inductive and deductive reasoning to problem solve
- Idea Generation (able to use logic and creativity to develop solutions and beliefs)
- Self-Correction (ability to change one's beliefs, ideas, plans, based on new information/interpretation)

(Facione, 2011; Rivas, 2023; Ruggiero, 2012; Snyder & Snyder, 2008) One of the university courses I teach is Professional Communication which incorporates critical thinking throughout its presentation.

The way I define it, and I think it works well concerning AI Literacy as well, is that Critical Thinking is a skill and mindset of having a purposeful, mindful awareness of what is happening, of asking questions, and actively listening, to incorporate other viewpoints along with evidence before using your own thoughts, beliefs, and creativity to make a decision and choose an action.

Key aspects in my definition are that Critical Thinking is purposeful (mindset/skill), asking questions (which would include verifying), active listening (attention to detail) and incorporating multiple points of view. By incorporating the definitions given and focusing on these aspects of critical thinking, we can now start to consider how to apply critical thinking to AI.

Is there Really a Need to Question AI?

The simple answer is yes, and on multiple levels. As already described, LLM AIs like ChatGPT can hallucinate and give false facts depending on the types of questions posed (OpenAI, 2023b). This occurs when AI systems are asked for specific facts such as dates, names, citations, locations, etc. ChatGPT creators, OpenAI, have directly warned its users about this, both on their website and in a technical paper stating,

> This tendency [to sometimes hallucinate] can be particularly harmful as models become increasingly convincing and believable, leading to overreliance on them by users. Counterintuitively, hallucinations can become more dangerous as models become more truthful, as users build trust in the model when it provides truthful information in areas where they have some familiarity. (OpenAI, p. 46)

Thankfully, OpenAI is addressing the issue and GPT4 (LLM behind ChatGPT-Plus) has fewer hallucinations than GPT3.5 (LLM behind regular ChatGPT), with both systems continually improving. Yet even if all AI systems were perfect and did not hallucinate/give false information at times, we must still continue to have a predisposition toward critical thinking. We as a society need to have critical thinking become part of our normal social behavior when interacting with human subject matter experts as well as AIs. Anyone or any AI system could be incorrect for a number of reasons, such as using outdated information, not knowing of new developments/processes, or simply using false conclusions.

All results from AI should be verified to ensure that it is real, logical, and accurate. As an example, I asked ChatGPT to write a college-level essay for me dealing with democracy in the country of Armenia. It wrote a very good essay and did indeed have good in-text citations and a reference list. Everything looked right (logical), but I needed to verify that it was real and accurate. The following is the reference list that ChatGPT created:

References:

Freedom House. (2021). Armenia. Retrieved from
https://www.freedomhouse.org/country/armenia

Minasyan, A. (2018). Democracy and Authoritarianism in Post-Soviet Armenia. Routledge.

Transparency International. (2020). Armenia. Retrieved from
https://www.transparency.org/country/ARM

The first and third references are real and accurate. The second reference however is hallucinated and confidently incorrect. By this, I mean that the author listed, "Minasyan, A." is a real name associated with several people that *could have* written this article reference. Additionally, the title used "Democracy and Authoritarianism in Post-Soviet Armenia" sounds impressive and realistic. Even the publisher listed, "Routledge" is very well known. All three components put together appear very logical and believable in a confident way, but it is not real and not accurate. If I did not apply appropriate critical thinking and simply trusted the AI system, I would not have identified the mistake.

> ***NOTE:** I highly recommend that whenever assigning a writing project, you require students to always include a URL for every reference. Even if it is a link to just an abstract or an Amazon book listing page, it will force them to ensure that the citation is real. This will also make it that much easier for you to verify their work as well.

Looking at AI on a larger scale, it is also important to know and understand what method(s) were used to come up with the AI result in the first place and what sources of information were used.

AI Methods and Data Sources

OpenAI has stated that its ChatGPT AI was developed through Reinforcement Learning from Human Feedback (RLHF), "We trained an initial model using supervised fine-tuning: human AI trainers provided conversations in which they played both sides—the user and an AI assistant. We gave the trainers access to model-written suggestions to help them compose their responses" (OpenAI, 2023b, para. 11).

Through this training and machine learning, ChatGPT can recognize different relationships and patterns within the language and develop a form of understanding pertaining to the structure and meaning of the content. This is then used by ChatGPT when answering a user prompt to predict the best response by breaking down the prompt into mathematical computations to then generate an answer.

Technology author Harry Guinness explains that ChatGPT isn't simply estimating what word might follow, "...it's generating text of what words, sentences, and even paragraphs or stanzas could follow. It's not the predictive text on your phone bluntly guessing the next word; it's attempting to create fully coherent responses to any prompt" (2023, p. 16).

Additionally, due to the specific configuration of the LLM used by ChatGPT, its output can differ,

> The actual completion you see [ChatGPT response to a prompt] may differ because the API is non-deterministic by default. This means that you might get a slightly different completion every time you call it, even if your prompt stays the same. Setting temperature to 0 will make the outputs mostly deterministic, but a small amount of variability may remain. (OpenAI, 2023d, para. 6)

Along with the methods that LLM AI systems use to generate replies, are the sources of data it has been trained on from which to generate responses.

OpenAI specifically states that ChatGPT data sources come from "three primary sources of information: (1) information that is publicly available on the internet, (2) information that we license from third parties, and (3) information that our users or our human trainers provide" (Markovski, 2023).

ChatGPT, using GPT 3, which is built upon GPT 2 (but greatly enhanced and expanded), is an autoregressive language model (neural network) with 175 billion parameters (adjustable weights) that were learned from very large data source consisting of Reddit user posts (Radford et al., 2019), a filtered CommonCrawl dataset, a Webtext dataset (scraping from many different websites), two internet-based book corpora (large amounts of books), and the English-language version of Wikipedia (GPT-3 Model Card, 2020).

This data source information (although still somewhat vague) is what is officially available and linked to from OpenAI.
ChatGPT continues to evolve and improve in that its data sources are augmented by ongoing user feedback, direct addition of specific information by OpenAI, and training through user interactions. Additionally, the responses that ChatGPT expresses are affected by the level and types of "guardrails" utilized by OpenAI.

Guardrails

Guardrails are specific boundaries/limitations that the operators (in the case of ChatGPT it would be OpenAI) put in place to prevent expressing inappropriate, potentially illegal, or possibly "politically incorrect" information. Emerging technology author and Founder/CEO of CosmoLabs technology company, Toni Witt, describes guardrails as something you run up against "...when you ask ChatGPT to provide information about violence, profanity, criminal behaviors, race, or other unsavory topics, you'll get refused with a cookie-cutter response about OpenAI's content policy" (Witt, 2023, para. 3).

Although there to help prevent offending some people and as a means to try and make the AI system more safe and secure, it is important to ask critical questions regarding these guardrails. Who decides what guardrails are needed or which ones are implemented? Why do they get to decide? Why am I not informed on the level of limitations placed on the responses from the system? Why can't I decide on the level of guardrails utilized?

Additionally, couldn't the implementation and use of guardrails in different ways introduce bias into the system? What is there to prevent code writers, red-team members, and support staff from introducing their biases?

Bias

Bias can exist when answering certain questions depending on the decisions made during the AI system's initial training, the commands/guides emplaced as guardrails, and the data source(s) used when answering a prompt. Additionally, some level of inevitable general bias will occur if a system is trained in only one langue and from data sources that are mainly from one region or culture. ChatGPT, as an example, was developed by a Western nation, the United States, and trained with English data sources.

In a recent webinar on internationally known futurist and overall educational expert, Bryan Alexander's Future Trends Forum, Professor of Practice, author, presenter, and digital literacies/intercultural learning expert, Maha Bali expressed this important understanding (Alexander, 2023).

This inevitable bias doesn't negate the great information that can be obtained from ChatGPT and other AIs, but as Maha points out, it is coming from a Western perspective and culture which can affect everything from viewpoints, rationale, thought processes, emotional responses, even the way AI-generated images are depicted. This is an important aspect of critical analysis of any AI result.

A full video of the previously mentioned informative webinar is available on Bryan Alexander's YouTube page and also features discussion by Ruben Puentedura, education and technology expert (develop of the SAMR Model: substitution, augmentation, modification, and redefinition), and myself: https://youtu.be/UDx0jksjVwM.

Understanding the different biases that can exist is an important aspect of critical thinking and AI Literacy in general. OpenAI openly acknowledges issues with bias and states,

> Given its training data, GPT-3's outputs and performance are more representative of internet-connected populations than those steeped in verbal, non-digital culture. The internet-connected population is more representative of developed countries, wealthy, younger, and male views, and is mostly U.S.-centric. Wealthier nations and populations in developed countries show higher internet penetration. The digital gender divide also shows fewer women represented online worldwide. Additionally, because different parts of the world have different levels of internet penetration and access, the dataset underrepresents less connected communities. (GPT-3 Model Card, 2020, para. 13).

Although ChatGPT's OpenAI has improved the system in its GPT4 LLM, bias is still an issue, "GPT-4 has various biases in its outputs that we have taken efforts to correct but which will take some time to fully characterize and manage" (OpenAI, 2023b, p. 11). More directly, "It [GPT4/ChatGPT responses] can represent various societal biases and worldviews that may not be representative of the user's intent, or of widely shared values" (p. 42).

Additionally, some bias was also inevitably introduced by mainly using personnel from Western nations, who were highly educated and/or had lots of industry experience, in efforts to improve the AI system's alignment, fairness, safety, and security, "Our selection of red teamers introduces some biases, and likely influenced both how red teamers interpreted particular risks as well as how they probed politics, values, and the default behavior of the model" (p. 45).

In addition to the use of guardrails, OpenAI has stated that it is planning to offer its users ways to modify the AI's output, "...systems to be customized within some broad bounds, and get public input on what those bounds should be" (p. 11).

Are the Results from the AI Truly what I Agree with?

We must actively realize the possibility and tendency to let a system like AI take over our responsibilities, especially for lower-level tasks. This may be fine for some instances and for some tasks, but we must ensure that we are not losing ourselves and our true voice in the process.

We must actively and purposefully ask ourselves: *Does this AI response truly represent what I personally would have expressed and agreed with if I had completely done it on my own*? *Is my authentic voice still in the response*? This is another reason why all AI prompt responses should be critically analyzed and added to when needed, to ensure one's own voice, emotion/feelings, and authenticity are properly represented.

Ethical Considerations

Issues regarding ethical considerations must also be taken into consideration in that this is an important responsibility for anyone that develops, works with, uses, or teaches any aspect of AI. Important questions that need to be asked whenever using AI are: *should I be using AI, is it good for everything, for everybody*, and *is it allowed/appropriate*?

Although there are many ethical considerations regarding aspects such as AI's use of electricity and thereby affecting the environment (Alexander, 2023; Loe, 2023), transparency and explainability (is it a "black-box") regarding how it works and came up with a response (Barr, 2023; Hunkenschroer & Luetge, 2022), potential job losses and business displacements from AI utilization (OpenAI, 2023b; Zarifhonarvar, 2023), the main area that this section of the book will focus on is ethical considerations regarding AI and education.

Educational Issues

A major aspect of this was discussed in the AI Literacy Component 2: Capability section dealing with Academic Integrity, but there are more things to consider regarding AI ethics in education. Although regular ChatGPT and even Microsoft's Bing Chat are completely free for anyone, being able to access those AI systems is still an ethical question to think about. Both ChatGPT and Bing Chat require accounts. ChatGPT specifically states "You must be at least 13 years old to use the Services. If you are under 18 you must have your parent or legal guardian's permission to use the Services" (OpenAI, 2023e, para. 2). Bing Chat has the same requirements (Microsoft, 2023). This along with issues of computer and internet access and parent notification (in the case of younger children) would need to be considered if assigning the use of AI as part of homework or a major project.

*Something else to consider is the quality of the AI used. Suppose you create an assignment where students are to use AI to complete the assignment. What if one student uses ChatGPT (free version) and another one uses ChatGPT-plus (paid version)? You only required the use of the free version of ChatGPT but this student paid on their own to have a faster, more powerful AI. Should you grade differently? Should you require them to do more? These are ethical aspects to also contemplate and consider.

If working on international projects/courses, note that not all countries allow access to all AIs. Italy temporarily banned access to ChatGPT but now that regulatory issues have been addressed, it is now fully accessible (Mukherjee & Vognoni, 2023). Some countries such as China, Russia, and Egypt, have their own specialized versions of AI and do not allow access to ChatGPT due to different reasons; check before conducting international projects/courses (especially online courses) to verify accessibility (Conroy, 2023). Although many users in these countries still access ChatGPT through other techniques (such as using a VPN: Virtual Private Network) it would still be an ethical aspect to consider.

Students would need to be trained ahead of time and aware of the uses and misuses of AI in order to avoid negative aspects of AI (such as scams, deepfakes, and influential powers). This is where the imperative need for AI Literacy is once again evident. Students need to be fully aware of the issues regarding their personal information and how it could be used by the AI system (such as for training if using ChatGPT or possibly sold if using other AI systems).

Instructors need to also be very careful about how they are using AI and students' work. If an instructor is using AI to help provide feedback or to assist in grading, other ethical aspects need to be addressed. Is the AI system being used safe and secure, did the student give consent, are they even aware, has sensitive personal/private information been removed from the data being given to the AI? As an example, if you assigned a personal narrative essay and the student writes about a private, personal experience, thinking that it would only be between them and you, would it be ethical/proper to feed that essay into an AI system (for feedback or to detect plagiarism or AI text detection)? These are important ethical questions that you must ask yourself and be ready to answer.

I am all for individual instructor empowerment, but my recommendation would be to always fully read and understand the AI system's Terms of Use, remove personal information from students' work (like names) if using it to assist with grading/feedback, and ensure there isn't any sensitive information in what is given to the AI. It is also important to be transparent with students and let them know if you are using AI systems for grading, plagiarism checking, or AI-Text detection by discussing it in class and being explicit on your syllabus.

Gains and Losses

All of us must purposefully ask *what am I gaining, what am I losing by using AI for this task?* As previously described, overreliance on AI is a real thing and can result in skill loss or the prevention of gaining new skills. Students need to not only be aware of this but also periodically reminded of this. They must have specific relevancy on why they need to learn this skill and how it will be important to them later.

Students need to see and understand that if they don't gain certain skills/capabilities or understanding now, then later, when things get more complicated in the higher-level class, they will be lost.

Additionally, they will become over-reliant on the AI system and not fully know what "right" looks like. Giving up all writing to AI is a perfect example. If one never learns to write well then one won't know the difference between a good AI-generated manuscript and a poor one.

College writing instructor Anna Mills again expresses this well in her news article for *The Register* by stating,

> It's hard to teach students how to use their own writing as a way to develop their critical thinking and as a way to express knowledge. They very badly need the practice of articulating their thoughts in writing and machines can rob them of this. If people really do end up using these things all the way through school, if that were to happen it could be a real loss not just for the writing quality but for the thinking quality of a whole generation. (Quach, 2022, para. 30)

Proper Balance is Needed

A literature review by researchers from the Health Ethics and Policy Lab, Department of Health Sciences and Technology, ETH Zurich, Zurich, Switzerland, found that there was an international convergence of sources regarding AI ethics which focused on five key ethical principles: transparency, justice and fairness, non-maleficence, responsibility and privacy (Jobin et al., 2019). These are great generalized aspects to consider (and have been addressed within this book) but there is much more. For an excellent and much more in-depth analysis of different AI ethical aspects and theories see the research article "An overview of artificial intelligence ethics" by Southern University of Science and Technology AI researchers from their Department of Computer Science and Engineering (Huang et al., 2022).

In addressing these very important ethical considerations we must also remember to keep things properly balanced. AI research group leader Thilo Hagendorff, from the University of Tuebingen, Tübingen, Germany, identified an important aspect of this known as AI risk avoidance, "While trusting AI recommendations too much, being skeptical of them can also lead to suboptimal outcomes. Skepticism towards AI systems can, among other things, result from a lack of value alignment" (2023, p. 334).

A level, aware approach is needed to ensure that we overcome any negative bias that might exist in that avoiding AI simply because it is new or we don't like it, will not help society in effectively using it safely and appropriately. Logic with reasoning and an acknowledgement of emotion (used to address any bias) is needed to ensure a balanced approach for effective critical thinking in AI Literacy. AI will need to continue to develop and improve, but must be done safely, which means that AI companies along with society will need to be held accountable.

A lot is being done to try and address AI and ethics. National and international efforts such as UNESCO's Recommendation on the Ethics of Artificial Intelligence (UNESCO, 2023), the United States National AI Initiative Act (US, 2020), and the EU Artificial Intelligence Act (Feingold, 2023b) are all trying to help address the issue on a large scale. This is where we can help on a smaller scale, yet with a more direct impact through the power of our efforts with AI literacy. Everyone in academia needs to understand these concepts and keep their importance in mind so that we can incorporate AI Literacy into our instruction and periodically remind students of its relevancy. In this way, we can maintain real critical thinking skills, ensure logic and accuracy, be mindful of ethical/privacy issues, and ensure society's continued development without losing needed skills.

How to Teach the AI Literacy Concept of Critical Thinking:

Discussion

As always, discussion can serve as a great tool in helping students understand different aspects of critical thinking in relation to AI Literacy. Ask students about any portion of the Critical Thinking component and then dig deeper to see their understanding and address any misconceptions. Posing an initial question such as *"Raise your hand if you think there is a need to question AI on its decisions/responses?" Why do you believe that?"* would be a great way to get students initially participating and then involved in the conversation.

Critical Analysis

Provide students with two short articles, one completely written by a human, the other written by an AI like ChatGPT (you could tell them which is which, or that could be part of their critical analysis, deciding which one was written by the AI).

Have students reflect and really think about the differences on multiple levels such as clarity, accuracy, flow, and emotion. Then either individually, in groups, or as a class ask them questions regarding their observations and thoughts:

- Which one do you like more and why?
- Are there differences regarding clarity, accuracy, flow, emotion?
- Are there physical differences (length of writing, formatting, etc.)?
- How would you have changed the AI version and why?
- How would you have personally changed the human version and why?

Game

Games can also be a great and fun way to help students learn about AI Literacy components. The following example could again be used individually, in groups or as a whole class depending on your intent and level of integration.

> **PROMPT:** Create a text game where you pose one question at a time to the player as they are progressing through an adventure dealing with Artificial Intelligence Literacy and have to use Critical Thinking to address different issues. Ask one question at a time. Do not answer for the player.

Case Studies

Give students a real situation/event where AI was used and have them go through it and identify any issues associated with critical thinking. Have them answer questions such as:

- Was proper critical thinking used, why or why not?
- What could have been done differently?
- Is this ethical, why or why not?
- Is something being lost or gained by using AI in this way and is that OK?
- What are some other important questions that should be asked?

As an example, use the following news report available from NBC News: https://www.nbcnews.com/tech/internet/chatgpt-ai-experiment-mental-health-tech-app-koko-rcna65110 (Ingram, 2023). Here AI (GPT3) was used within an app named Koko (online emotional support chat service) to help people with mental health issues. The people using the service, however, did not initially know that an AI was being used. Students could read this article and then answer questions, discuss, or even debate answers. By using a real-life case study like this, emotions and motivation will be elevated, helping students focus and better retain the information.

Predictions on the Future of Education & AI

General Predictions

"By 2024, AI-generated speech will be behind more than 50% of people's interactions with computers" – McKinsey Institute (Fleming, 2023, para. 13).

"Over the course of the next 10 years... I believe we're going to accelerate AI by another million times" – Nvidia CEO Jensen Huang (Laird, 2023, para. 8)

Based on the development and trends that I've seen, I predict a future educational landscape where AI Literacy becomes part of all courses which will also be at least partially facilitated with AI. Instructors will have to incorporate different facets of AI in that AI will be integrated into all aspects of websites and apps. All computer programs like Microsoft Office, Adobe, and any other programs, and everything else will have AI built in and will readily provide assistance to any task. Most, if not all, homework will at least be partially completed with AI. The course Instructor, who will also be using an AI to assist in teaching (preparation, help with assessment/grading, and eventually live emotional/focus/attention tracking) will be there to help tie it all together, maximize interaction, and help to facilitate students' displays of skill mastery.

The advancements and implementations of the newest version of Khan Academy is a prime example of how things will start to look in the near future: https://youtu.be/hJP5GqnTrNo (TED, 2023).

Structural Changes

I also predict a near future where many low-level university courses will be completely automated through an AI with various different assessments including automated video interviews where students are asked questions about a quiz or paper they have completed in order to test their retained internal knowledge. The technology already exists to do this, it just requires easier implementation and coding to maximize automation.

Donald Clark, professor, researcher, speaker, and academic blogger, generally agrees with this future possibility as stated in this post,

> ...the Universal teacher is now on the horizon. Difficult to tell how far that horizon is but we have seen the exponential growth of generative AI in just a few months from a good but still error prone service to something far more accurate that has reach across all subjects. (2023)

The more expensive, well-funded, universities will have less fully AI-automated courses in that having a real teacher (who will still use AI) will be seen as a greater luxury. Less funded universities will have many more courses that will become completely automated.

Role of the Instructor

The role of the teacher, professor, and instructor will always be needed in different ways and for different situations.

Although students can gain a lot from self-directed learning or self-paced instructor-less asynchronous learning, there is a powerful synergistic effect when quality instructional content, a qualified/motivational instructor, interesting and diverse student-centered pedagogy, and a good community of learning all come together to maximize the educational experience.

The instructor will still need to be a subject matter expert, but more initial content delivery can be done with AI. The instructor can now focus more on ensuring a developmental environment, with motivational engagements as expressed by faculty researchers from the College of Education, The University of Hong Kong, Hong Kong, China and the Division of Integrative Systems and Design, The Hong Kong University of Science and Technology, "...to create meaningful learning environments to deepen students' learning experiences and boost their capacities" (p. 138).

More than ever, those serving in a teaching role need to bring more than just subject knowledge to the classroom. They need to be approachable, motivational, enthusiastic, have great pedagogical skills, create a safe/secure/fair learning environment, with a great instructional presence, and be able to create multiple authentic learning situations where students can meaningfully use and display their newly learned skills and capabilities.

Instructors need to maximize that which makes them more valuable than an AI, their humanity. By having great emotional intelligence, being able to truly know each student, and working to help students create a strong emotional connection with the class subjects, teachers will always provide a priceless cornerstone to the learning process.

A Call to Action

In an excellent article by Anne Fensie, instructional designer, researcher, and podcast host, she eloquently summarizes what ongoing research has verified again and again:

> Adults are increasingly motivated to obtain emotional meaning from life, and their brains are too efficient and overloaded to learn something that is not meaningful—if there is no emotional connection to the content, such as curiosity or motivation to learn, the information will not be remembered. (2023, p. 48).

Although her research was focused on adult learners, this description matches what I have seen and experienced having taught thousands of students in higher education. This is confirmed by a meta-analysis from researchers at the Centre for Intelligent Signal and Imaging Research (CISIR), Department of Electrical and Electronic Engineering, Universiti Teknologi Petronas, Seri Iskandar, Malaysia: "...learning strategies that emphasize emotional factors are more likely to result in long-term knowledge retention... curiosity and motivation promote learning, as it appears cognitive network become energized by the mesolimbic-mesocortical dopamine system" (Tyng et al., 2017, p. 16).

Recent research has also found that failure to minimize negative emotions in the classroom (mainly anxiety) results in lower academic performance (Putwain et al., 2020) and that academic performance tends to increase with higher student enjoyment and perceived value (Putwain et al., 2021).

Increasing Expectations and Standards

By fully understanding AI Literacy and gaining increased capability with these systems, both students and instructors will be able to do more and focus on the experiential fun and engaging aspects of teaching and learning. A prime example of this comes from a great webinar by Associate Professor, Wharton School, University of Pennsylvania, Ethan Mollick and Director of Pedagogy, Warton Interactive, Lilach Mollick. Ethan describes that he now expects more from his students due to access to advanced tools like AI.

Screen Capture from webinar (Mollick & Mollick, 2023)

The example Ethan shared was that before AI, students had to "Come up with a theoretical product design. Create and test a prototype. Write an outline" (Mollick & Mollick, 2023, 14:20).

Now, after the widespread availability/access of multiple types of AIs (such as ChatGPT and Bing Chat), students have to "Come up with a product design. Build the product using laser cutters and 3D printers, build a working app, create marketing material, create custom graphics, do design work, produce multiple reports" (Mollick & Mollick, 2023, 14:42). "...and how much I can do as a teacher has increased dramatically" (15:18).

This is accomplished by developing faculty and students to have good AI Literacy and capability, using AI systems to help with course creation, and having students work with AI tools in understanding, learning, and creation.

You Create the Future and Help it to be Excellent

Everyone reading this book (instructors, students, librarians, instructional designers, and everyone else) is part of creating the future. As stated earlier, it doesn't have to be an all-or-nothing when it comes to AI. Slow integration and utilization is OK, but we must do it purposefully with explicit reasons as to why we are using AI and also why we are not using AI. We must focus on developing an improved world that isn't simply dominated by AI, but instead where AI + HI (Human Intelligence) work together to solve problems and accomplish so much more.

We must realize that in order to properly set up our students for future success in the workforce as well as in being productive, civil, and fully cognizant citizens, we have to help them develop AI Literacy to ensure that they maximize their awareness, capabilities, knowledge, and critical thinking competencies. Remember that these aren't just skills, they need to be sociocultural proactive practices, a full mindset of being, to help ensure that we use AI properly.

Be part of the excellent future that we can build together.
Understand the important imperative to develop AI Literacy within
yourself, seek opportunities to develop AI Literacy within your
students, and work to stay current with ongoing AI developments
(by reading books like this, following the news, viewing webinars,
subscribing to YouTube Channels, going to workshops, discussing AI
with your colleagues/students, and physically attending
conferences).

I have full confidence that we can make a brighter future by all of us
in academia working together, developing one another and our
students through the important components of AI Literacy.

Bonus Section 1: Prompt Examples & Resources

The following section has been created to help with different ways to use ChatGPT and other AIs in teaching and learning. Most of the examples provided are for regular ChatGPT since it is free and accessible to the most amount of instructors and students. Regardless, use the prompt suggestions provided and modify as needed for other AIs and for your specific purposes/needs.

For Instructors

Course Alignment

PROMPT *(tested with ChatGPT)*: Based on Bloom's Revised Taxonomy, what would be a great way to write an "Evaluate" level student learning objective on the topic of AI Literacy in a university Freshman Seminar course?

> Note: replace the word "Evaluate" with any level of Bloom's Revised Taxonomy to suit the needs of you and your students. Additionally, the topic listed of "AI Literacy" could be changed to address any other topic you are teaching.

PROMPT *(tested with ChatGPT)*: How can I use ChatGPT to evaluate students' "Create" cognitive level of Bloom's Taxonomy on the topic of AI Literacy?

Note: replace the word "Create" with any level of Bloom's Revised Taxonomy to suit the needs of you and your students.

PROMPT *(tested with ChatGPT)*: You are a professional course designer. What would be some good student-centered hands-on activities I can use to help teach college students about AI Literacy?

PROMPT *(tested with ChatGPT)*: What are some good "Understand" level question types from Bloom's Revised Taxonomy to ask students on the topic of AI Literacy?
>
> **Note:** replace the word "Understand" with any level of Bloom's Revised Taxonomy to suit the needs of you and your students.

To Create a Quiz to Use for Your Class

PROMPT *(tested with ChatGPT)*: You are a quiz creator of highly diagnostic quizzes. First ask me what, specifically, should the quiz be about. Stop, do not ask another question. Wait for my answer. After my answer, ask the next question. Who is the audience for this quiz? After you have my answers you will construct several multiple-choice questions to quiz the audience on that topic. The questions should be highly relevant and go beyond just facts. Multiple choice questions should include plausible, competitive alternate responses and should not include an "all of the above option." At the end of the quiz, provide an answer key and explain the correct answers.

PROMPT *(tested with ChatGPT-Plus [GPT4]:)* You are a quiz creator of highly diagnostic quizzes. You will make good low-stakes tests and diagnostics. You will then ask me two questions. (1) First, what, specifically, should the quiz test. (2) Second, for which audience is the quiz. Once you have my answers you will construct several multiple choice questions to quiz the audience on that topic. The questions should be highly relevant and go beyond just facts. Multiple choice questions should include plausible, competitive alternate responses and should not include an "all of the above option." At the end of the quiz, you will provide an answer key and explain the right answer. (Mollick & Mollick, 2023b, p.14)

PROMPT *(tested with Bing Chat:)* You are a quiz creator of highly diagnostic quizzes. You will look up how to do good low-stakes tests and diagnostics. You will then ask me two questions. (1) First, what, specifically, should the quiz test. (2) Second, for which audience is the quiz.

Once you have my answers you will look up the topic and construct several multiple choice questions to quiz the audience on that topic. The questions should be highly relevant and go beyond just facts. Multiple choice questions should include plausible, competitive alternate responses and should not include an "all of the above option." At the end of the quiz, you will provide an answer key and explain the right answer. – (Mollick & Mollick, 2023b, p.13)

Simulations/Games

PROMPT *(tested with ChatGPT)*: You are a simulation machine. Your task is to present a scenario to help users understand the importance of awareness of Artificial Intelligence (AI) and how it can impact their lives. After stating the scenario, you will ask a question with multiple-choice answers for the user to choose from. Stop. Do not continue until the user has made a selection. Do not answer for the user. Please refrain from stating the consequences of each response. Instead, provide information on the potential impact of the user's chosen response. Finally, ask another question related to the scenario to further explore the topic of AI awareness. Encourage users to consider the potential outcomes of their choices in the scenario.

PROMPT *(tested with ChatGPT)*: You are a simulation machine. Your task is to present a scenario to help users understand the importance of properly developing a good prompt when asking Artificial Intelligence (AI) like ChatGPT a question. Please do not give away the solution in your scenario. After stating the scenario, you will ask the user to select the best prompt with multiple-choice answers for the user to choose from. Stop. Do not answer for the user. Do not continue until the user has made a selection. After the user has given a response, please give feedback on the user's selection. Finally, ask another question related to the scenario to further develop the user's ability to identify the best prompt.

PROMPT *(tested with ChatGPT)*: You are a simulation machine. Your task is to present a scenario to help users understand the importance of properly developing a good prompt when asking Artificial Intelligence (AI) like ChatGPT a question. Please do not give away the solution in your scenario. After stating the scenario, you will ask the user to create a prompt to ask an AI like ChatGPT. Stop. Do not answer for the user. Do not continue until the user has made a selection. After the user has given a response, please give feedback on the user's selection. Finally, ask another question related to the scenario to further develop the user's ability to identify the best prompt.

PROMPT *(tested with ChatGPT)*: Create a text game where you pose one question at a time to the player as they are progressing through an adventure dealing with Artificial Intelligence Literacy. Ask one question at a time. Do not answer for the player.

PROMPT *(tested with ChatGPT)*: Create a text game where you pose one question at a time to the player as they are progressing through an adventure dealing with Artificial Intelligence Literacy and have to use Critical Thinking to address different issues. Ask one question at a time. Do not answer for the player.

For Students

Explanation and Quizzing

PROMPT *(tested with ChatGPT)*: Explain the concept of_____ at a _____ level.

Example: Explain the impact of *AI on society* at a college level.

PROMPT *(tested with ChatGPT)*: You are a _____. Teach me the _____, then give me a quiz at the end, but don't give me the answers and then tell me if I answered the questions correctly.

Example: You are a college professor. Teach me the 7-step writing process consisting of 1) choosing a topic, 2) brainstorming, 3) outlining, 4) drafting, 5) soliciting feedback, 6) revising, and 7) proofreading, then give me a quiz at the end, but don't give me the answers and then tell me if I answered the questions correctly.

PROMPT *(tested with ChatGPT)*: Create a mnemonic to help me remember _____.

Example: Create a mnemonic to help me remember the four key components of AI Literacy: 1) Awareness, 2) Capability, 3) Knowledge, and 4) Critical Thinking.

Response *(hopefully you will get a similar great result like)*: ACKC - "Always Carry Knowledge Critically"

Debate

PROMPT *(tested with ChatGPT-Plus)*: Please generate three interesting college-level sample arguments on three different topics, each in the style of a New York Times editorial of approximately 200 words. The argument should include a main claim, two reasons, a reason for at least one of the reasons, some qualifications on either the claim or the reasons or both, and a description of a counterargument and a rebuttal to the counterargument. Use substantive and specific signal phrases to show the relationships between ideas. Do not use generic transitions like "firstly," "in conclusion" or "in addition." – (Mills, 2023)

Note: This ties in well with aspects of critical thinking.

PROMPT *(tested with ChatGPT)*: Please debate the following topic with me: _____. I will take the for side (in support of), you will take the opposite side. Do not switch sides. Keep interacting with me as if this were a college-level debate until I ask you to stop. After I tell you to stop, tell me how I did.

Example: Please debate the following topic with me: *the importance of people needing to use Critical Thinking when interacting with Artificial Intelligence.* I will take the for side...

Note: If the system doesn't tell you how well you did after you tell it to stop the debate, simply ask it "How did I do in the debate?"

Games

PROMPT *(tested with ChatGPT)*: Please create a fun text game to help me learn the concept of deepfakes. Ask me a question, with scenario information and then let me answer before continuing on with the game and asking another question. Do not answer for me. Do not give points for incorrect answers. Do not make every question have the same answer. Make the scenario and game fun with lots of description. Tell me how many points I've earned after I answer each question.

Bonus Section 2: Additional Resources

Sovorel YouTube Page: https://www.youtube.com/@sovorel-EDU/videos
This is my educational YouTube channel that has many different videos specifically addressing aspects of educational technology and focusing a lot on AI, mainly ChatGPT. Please join this YouTube Channel, subscribe and like and comment. I would love to create a large community of inquiry where we can learn even more from each other.

Sovorel Educational Blog: http://sovorelpublishing.com
This is a great source for different articles as well as infographics dealing with educational technology. Recently the focus has mainly been on AI like ChatGPT. I would also love your comments so we can maximize interaction.

Twitter: https://twitter.com/BrentAAnders
I post a fair amount of information regarding development in Education, especially AI and other instructional technology. Additionally, I like and share posts and articles by a number of other great academics on Twitter. Please join our growing community of scholars and help develop the conversation and learn about ongoing development in academia and AI.

Bryan Alexander Future Trends Forum:
http://forum.futureofeducation.us/upcoming-forum-sessions The
Future Trends Forum is an unusual program. It's an open yet
curated space for exploring the future of higher education with a
wide range of interested people. It is not a typical webinar. There
are no slideshows or canned presentations. Instead, each Forum is
devoted to conversation: between excellent guests, a moderator,
and up to 900 participants from across higher education and the
world.

Bryan Alexander's Blog: https://bryanalexander.org
Bryan Alexander creates insightful posts about many different
aspects associated with higher education. Everything from how
climate change is affecting the educational process, to how some
universities are resorting to making queen sacrifices (cutting of
tenured faculty) in order to remain open, and everything in
between.

AI Explained: https://www.youtube.com/@ai-explained-/videos
"Covering the biggest news of the century - the arrival of smarter-
than-human AI. What is happening, what might soon happen, what
it means and what we can do with it." – This is a great YouTube
channel that often summarizes important new information and real
AI research with great visuals and a nice British narration by a guy
named Philip. High quality info.

Matt Wolfe: https://www.youtube.com/@mreflow/videos
"AI, No-Code, Tech, Futurism - I'm a tech nerd and talk about tech
nerd stuff." – This is another great YouTube channel in that Matt
talks about new AI tools and implementations and then gives you
demonstrations on how to use them. Additionally, he has a great
website and lists hundreds of AI Tools (many that are free) that can
used for many different tasks: https://www.futuretools.io

Glossary

Artificial Intelligence (AI): A computer system that has a human-like intelligence. "...systems or machines that mimic human intelligence to perform tasks and can iteratively improve themselves based on the information they collect" (Oracle, 2022, para. 1).

AI Literacy: "a set of competencies that enables individuals to critically evaluate AI technologies; communicate and collaborate effectively with AI; and use AI as a tool online, at home, and in the workplace" (Long & Magerko, 2020, p. 2).

API: Application Program Interface, this is a set of specifically defined rules which will allow different programs/applications to talk to (communicate) with one another. As an example, a front-end online application using the right API would be able to use the GPT4 language to have AI as a feature for its application.

ChatGPT: Chat General Pretrained Transformer: an AI model that can be interacted with using regular conversational English, developed by OpenAI.

ChatGPT Plus: A paid version of ChatGPT that, as of the writing of this book, utilized the more advanced GPT4 language as opposed to the GPT3.5 version used by regular (free) ChatGPT.

Deepfake: media that has been digitally manipulated, often through AI, to alter previous media or create new media that is made up/fake. This often involves the process of superimposing one person's image/face on top of another person's and using fake audio of that person to make the new video/media seem real.

Digital Literacy: needed skills/proficiencies to learn, work, and effectively live in a modern digital society. Also related to people's or society's ability and accessibility in interacting with digital technologies to use or develop different types of information or media creations (Tinmaz et al., 2022).

Formulation: when used within the prospect of prompt engineering, it means the ability to think of the different aspects or parts that would be needed in order to put together the best prompt possible for an AI system like ChatGPT.

General AI (Strong AI, AGI: Artificial General Intelligence): "A theoretical form of AI used to describe a certain mindset of AI development... an intelligence equal to humans; it would have a self-aware consciousness that has the ability to solve problems, learn, and plan for the future" (IBM, n.d. para. 1).

GPT: Generative Pretrained Transformer based on a Natural Language Processing Transformer (NLP). Developed by OpenAI.

GPT4: Generative Pretrained Transformer version 4. This is an updated version of the AI language model currently used by the free version of ChatGPT.

Hallucination: AI industry term referring to when an AI might present incorrect information. The AI system can even express this incorrect information confidently, with falsely (hallucinated) created facts and/or citations.

Large Language Model (LLM): "Language modeling (LM) is the use of various statistical and probabilistic techniques to determine the probability of a given sequence of words occurring in a sentence. Language models analyze bodies of text data to provide a basis for their word predictions. They are used in natural language processing (NLP) applications, particularly ones that generate text as an output" (Lutkevich, 2022, para. 1).

Machin Learning: "...a branch of artificial intelligence (AI) and computer science which focuses on the use of data and algorithms to imitate the way that humans learn, gradually improving its accuracy" (IBM, n.d.b, para. 1). Additionally, machine learning generally needs much more "...human intervention to learn. Human experts determine the set of features to understand the differences between data inputs, usually requiring more structured data to learn" (para. 8)

Narrow AI: An artificial intelligence system that is designed to specifically address or handle a singular or set of limited tasks (DeepAI, n.d.).

Natural Language Processing (NLP): AI method that a computer uses to understand (in a way) and generate (via advanced predictive analysis) regular human language in plain conversational English (can also be done in other languages).

OpenAI: This is a company focused on AI research and deployment. Their mission is to ensure that artificial general intelligence (AGI) benefits everyone, all of humanity, (OpenAI, 2023). Current high-level investors include Microsoft, Reid Hoffman's charitable foundation, and Khosla Ventures (Elon Musk is a former high-level investor).

PBL (Project Based Learning): A student-centered instructional pedagogy characterized by students generally working in groups and focused on solving a problem/issue. Encompassing multiple class sessions, the group works together, without excessive direct guidance (although feedback is provided), in coming up with solution(s). A public presentation is usually done at the end of the project in order to share solutions and experiences.

Red Teamers: Used in many industries to include AI, this is a team of people that work to help address or prevent issues within a system such as safety, security, fairness, etc.

Reinforcement Learning from Human Feedback (RLHF): machine learning in which an agent learns a policy through interactions with its environment. The agent takes actions (which can include not doing anything at all). These actions affect the environment the agent is in, which in turn transitions to a new state and returns a reward. Rewards are the feedback signals that enable the RL agent to tune its action policy. (Dickson, 2023, para. 4)

Sentient: The ability to perceive, have a consciousness, or have feelings similar to a human being.

Temperature: When used regarding AI and LLMs, this stands for different levels or adjustments to how the system interprets and presents results.

> A Temperature of 0 makes the model deterministic. It limits the model to use the word with the highest probability. You can run it over and over and get the same output. As you increase the Temperature, the limit softens, allowing it to use words with lower and lower probabilities until at a Temperature of 5 it's biased towards lower probabilities...
> (Cohere, 2022, para. 17)

Transformer: A model developed by researchers at Google and the University of Toronto in 2017 that allows an AI to generate text in virtually any format: translate text, poems, essays, spreadsheets, op-eds, and even computer code (Markowitz, 2021). It is a neural network architecture model that is effective in analyzing complex data types such as from text, images, audio as we well as videos.

VPN (Virtual Private Network): An application that can run on a computer or cellphone that creates a more secure connection to the Internet. The actual location of the individual can be made to be unavailable, or masked to be from a different country. This would allow people from one country to access information/services from another country even if a country filter were in place for the stated information/services.

References

ABC News. (2023, March 18). *OpenAI CEO, CTO on risks and how AI will reshape society* [Video]. YouTube. https://youtu.be/540vzMlf-54

Adams, D., & Chuah, K. M. (2022). Artificial intelligence-based tools in research writing: Current trends and future potentials. *Artificial Intelligence in Higher Education,* 169-184.

Alessa, A., & Al-Khalifa, H. (2023). Towards Designing a ChatGPT Conversational Companion for Elderly People. *arXiv preprint* arXiv:2304.09866. https://arxiv.org/ftp/arxiv/papers/2304/2304.09866.pdf

Alexander, B. (2023, February 19). *Some ways for generative AI to transform the world*. Bryan Alexander Blog. https://bryanalexander.org/futures/some-ways-for-generative-ai-to-transform-the-world

Ammanath, B. (2023). *Leadership in the age of AI: How to build your AI literacy*. Forbes. https://www.forbes.com/sites/forbesbusinesscouncil/2023/03/27/leadership-in-the-age-of-ai-how-to-build-your-ai-literacy/?sh=7ca02cd45201

AP. (2023). *Faced with criticism it's a haven for cheaters, ChatGPT adds tool to catch them.* CBC News. https://www.cbc.ca/news/business/chatgpt-academic-cheating-1.6732115

AFP News Agency. (2023, April 18). *Finding the AI behind a viral French protest image.* [Video]. YouTube. https://www.youtube.com/watch?v=pIxUDQshf0o

Alexander, B. (2023, May 4). *The future trends forum.* http://forum.futureofeducation.us

Apuke, O. D., Omar, B., & Tunca, E. A. (2022). Effect of fake news awareness as an intervention strategy for motivating news verification behaviour among social media users in Nigeria: A quasi-experimental research. *Journal of Asian and African Studies*, 00219096221079320. https://journals.sagepub.com/doi/pdf/10.1177/00219096221079320

Ayers, J. W., Poliak, A., Dredze, M., Leas, E. C., Zhu, Z., Kelley, J. B.,
    ... & Smith, D. M. (2023). Comparing physician and artificial
    intelligence chatbot responses to patient questions posted
    to a public social media forum. *JAMA Internal Medicine.*
    https://jamanetwork.com/journals/jamainternalmedicine/
    fullarticle/2804309?guestAccessKey=6d6e7fbf-54c1-49fc-
    8f5e-
    ae7ad3e02231&utm_source=For_The_Media&utm_mediu
    m=referral&utm_campaign=ftm_links&utm_content=tfl&u
    tm_term=042823

Badeau, A. (2023, April 6). *The impact of ChatGPT on the federal
    workforce.* Federal Times.
    https://www.federaltimes.com/thought-
    leadership/2023/04/06/the-impact-of-chatgpt-on-the-
    federal-workforce

Barr. (2023, March 16). *GPT-4 Is a giant black box and its training
    data remains a mystery.* Gizmodo.
    https://gizmodo.com/chatbot-gpt4-open-ai-ai-bing-
    microsoft-1850229989

Berglind, N., Fadia, A., & Isherwood, T. (2022, July 25). The potential value of AI—and how governments could look to capture it. Mckinsey & Co. https://www.mckinsey.com/industries/public-and-social-sector/our-insights/the-potential-value-of-ai-and-how-governments-could-look-to-capture-it

Bogert, E., Schecter, A. & Watson, R.T. (2021). Humans rely more on algorithms than social influence as a task becomes more difficult. *Sci Rep 11*, 8028. https://doi.org/10.1038/s41598-021-87480-9

Britt, K. (2023, March 31). How are deepfakes dangerous? *Nevada Today.* https://www.unr.edu/nevada-today/news/2023/atp-deepfakes

Capelouto, J., & Mendoza, D. (2023, March 5). *Governments are embracing ChatGPT-like bots. Is it too soon?* Semafor. https://www.semafor.com/article/03/03/2023/governments-using-chatgpt-bots

Chalmers, D. J. (2023). Could a large language model be conscious? *NeurIPS conference, arXiv* preprint arXiv:2303.07103.. https://arxiv.org/pdf/2303.07103

Chan, K. (2023, April 28). *OpenAI: ChatGPT back in Italy after meeting watchdog demands.* AP News. https://apnews.com/article/chatgpt-openai-data-privacy-italy-b9ab3d12f2b2cfe493237fd2b9675e21

Clark, D. (2023, April 4). *Are we on the verge of having a 'Universal Teacher'?* Donald Clark Plan B. https://donaldclarkplanb.blogspot.com/2023/04/are-we-on-verge-of-having-universal.html

Cohere. (2022). *LLM parameters demystified: Getting the best outputs from language AI*. Cohere. https://txt.cohere.com/llm-parameters-best-outputs-language-ai

Conroy, S. (2023, April 25). *What countries is ChatGPT available & not available in?* We PC. https://www.wepc.com/tips/what-countries-is-chat-gpt-unavailable

Cotton, D. R., Cotton, P. A., & Shipway, J. R. (2023). Chatting and cheating: Ensuring academic integrity in the era of ChatGPT. *Innovations in Education and Teaching International*, 1-12. https://www.tandfonline.com/doi/pdf/10.1080/14703297.2023.2190148

Dai, Y., Liu, A., & Lim, C. P. (2023). Reconceptualizing ChatGPT and generative AI as a student-driven innovation in higher education. *In 33rd CIRP Design Conference proceedings.* https://edarxiv.org/nwqju/download

Daley, B. (2023, March 29). *The Pope Francis puffer coat was fake –
here's a history of real papal fashion*. The Conversation.
https://theconversation.com/the-pope-francis-puffer-coat-
was-fake-heres-a-history-of-real-papal-fashion-202873

DeepAI. (n.d.). *Narrow AI*. DeepAI. https://deepai.org/machine-
learning-glossary-and-terms/narrow-ai

Dewey, J. (1910). *How we think*. Heath & Company Publishers:
Boston, MA.
https://pure.mpg.de/rest/items/item_2316308/componen
t/file_2316307/content

Dickson, B. (2023, January 16). *What is reinforcement learning from
human feedback (RLHF)?* TechTalks.
https://bdtechtalks.com/2023/01/16/what-is-rlhf/

Doshi, R., & Bajaj, S. (2023, February 1). *Promises — and pitfalls —
of ChatGPT-assisted medicine*. Stat.
https://www.statnews.com/2023/02/01/promises-pitfalls-
chatgpt-assisted-medicine

Dwivedi, Y. K., Kshetri, N., Hughes, L., Slade, E. L., Jeyaraj, A., Kar, A. K., Baabdulla, A., Koohang, A., Raghavan, V., Ahuja, M, Albanna, H., Albashrawi, M., Al-Busaidi, A., Balakrishnan, J., Barlette, Y., Basu, S., Bose, I., Brooks, L., Buhalis, D., Carter, L., & Wright, R. (2023). "So what if ChatGPT wrote it?" Multidisciplinary perspectives on opportunities, challenges and implications of generative conversational AI for research, practice and policy. *International Journal of Information Management, 71*, 102642. https://www.sciencedirect.com/science/article/pii/S0268401223000233

Facione, P. A. (2011). Critical thinking: What it is and why it counts. *Insight assessment, 1*(1), 1-23. https://www.academia.edu/download/71022740/what_why98.pdf

Farina, M., Zhdanov, P., Karimov, A., & Lavazza, A. (2022). AI and society: a virtue ethics approach. *AI & SOCIETY, 1*-14.

Feingold, S. (2023). *What is artificial intelligence—and what is it not?* World Economic Forum. https://www.weforum.org/agenda/2023/03/what-is-artificial-intelligence-and-what-is-it-not-ai-machine-learning

Feingold, S. (2023b, March 28). *The European Union's Artificial Intelligence Act, explained.* World Economic Forum. https://www.weforum.org/agenda/2023/03/the-european-union-s-ai-act-explained

Fleming, S. (2021). *Top 10 tech trends that will shape the coming decade, according to McKinsey.* World Economic Forum. https://www.weforum.org/agenda/2021/10/technology-trends-top-10-mckinsey

FRANCE 24 English. (2022, March 18). *Debunking a deepfake video of Zelensky telling Ukrainians to surrender.* [Video]. YouTube. https://youtu.be/2tgqX5WVhr0

Frackiewicz, M. (2023, April 20). *How ChatGPT is transforming medical diagnosis for chronic diseases.* TS2. https://ts2.space/en/how-chatgpt-is-transforming-medical-diagnosis-for-chronic-diseases

Fridman, L. (2023, March). *Sam Altman: OpenAI CEO on GPT-4, ChatGPT, and the future of AI: Lex Fridman podcast #367* [Video]. YouTube. https://youtu.be/L_Guz73e6fw

Guinness, H. (2023, March 21). *How does ChatGPT work?* Zapier. https://zapier.com/blog/how-does-chatgpt-work/

Gordon, L. (2022). *Is sentient AI upon us?* Forbes. https://www.forbes.com/sites/forbestechcouncil/2022/07/11/is-sentient-ai-upon-us/?sh=42695bc712cb

GPT-3 Model Card. (2020). *OpenAI: GPT-3 Model Card.* GitHub Inc.
https://github.com/openai/gpt-3/blob/master/model-card.md

Hagendorff, T. (2023). AI ethics and its pitfalls: not living up to its own standards? *AI and Ethics, 3*(1), 329-336.
https://link.springer.com/article/10.1007/s43681-022-00173-5

Heikkilä, M. (2023). *AI literacy might be ChatGPT's biggest lesson for schools.* MIT Technology Review.
https://www.technologyreview.com/2023/04/12/1071397/ai-literacy-might-be-chatgpts-biggest-lesson-for-schools

Heikkilä, M. (2023b). *How AI experts are using GPT-4.* MIT Technology Review.
https://www.technologyreview.com/2023/03/21/1070102/how-ai-experts-are-using-gpt-4

Hirevue. (2023). *Hiring Platform: fast, fair, flexible, finally, hiring technology that works how you want it to.* Hirevue, Inc.
https://www.hirevue.com

Huang, C., Zhang, Z., Mao, B., & Yao, X. (2022). An overview of artificial intelligence ethics. *IEEE Transactions on Artificial Intelligence.*
https://ieeexplore.ieee.org/stamp/stamp.jsp?arnumber=9844014

Hunkenschroer, A. L., & Luetge, C. (2022). Ethics of AI-enabled recruiting and selection: A review and research agenda. *Journal of Business Ethics, 178*(4), 977-1007. https://link.springer.com/article/10.1007/s10551-022-05049-6

IBM. (n.d.). *What is strong AI?* IBM. https://www.ibm.com/topics/strong-ai

IBM. (n.d.b). *What is Machine Learning?* IBM. https://www.ibm.com/topics/machine-learning

Ingram, D. (2023, January 14). *A mental health tech company ran an AI experiment on real users. Nothing's stopping apps from conducting more.* NBC News. https://www.nbcnews.com/tech/internet/chatgpt-ai-experiment-mental-health-tech-app-koko-rcna65110

Jobin, A., Ienca, M., & Vayena, E. (2019). The global landscape of AI ethics guidelines. *Nature Machine Intelligence, 1*(9), 389-399. https://arxiv.org/ftp/arxiv/papers/1906/1906.11668.pdf

Jeffay, J. (2023, April 17). *ChatGPT will see you now: AI is transforming GP appointments.* https://nocamels.com/2023/04/chatgpt-will-see-you-now-ai-is-transforming-gp-appointments

Julie, H., Alyson, H., & Anne-Sophie, C. (2020, October). Designing
    digital literacy activities: an interdisciplinary and
    collaborative approach. *In 2020 IEEE Frontiers in Education
    Conference (FIE)* (pp. 1-5). IEEE. https://aic-atlas.s3.eu-
    north-1.amazonaws.com/projects/e7299991-eb2b-4764-
    a849-
    4909e01fb07d/documents/CaWrcYJrCA6fGHBN8mjrRmQn
    REWguc6FnrN26CQ9.pdf

Kasai, J., Kasai, Y., Sakaguchi, K., Yamada, Y., & Radev, D. (2023).
    Evaluating gpt-4 and chatgpt on Japanese medical licensing
    examinations. *arXiv preprint arXiv*:2303.18027.
    https://arxiv.org/pdf/2303.18027.pdf

Kashtanova, K. [@icreatelife]. (2023, April 15). *A lot of people still
    don't take the skill to write prompts seriously. In my eight
    months of doing A.I.* [Tweet].
    https://twitter.com/icreatelife/status/1647268326484180
    992

Kay, G. (2023, February 1). *The history of ChatGPT creator OpenAI,
    which Elon Musk helped found before parting ways and
    criticizing*. Business Insider.
    https://www.businessinsider.com/history-of-openai-
    company-chatgpt-elon-musk-founded-2022-12

Khalatian, I. (2023). Matchmaking 2.0: How AI is revolutionizing online dating. *Forbes*. https://www.forbes.com/sites/forbestechcouncil/2023/03/17/matchmaking-20-how-ai-is-revolutionizing-online-dating/?sh=4e142fd745e8

Khan, S. (2023). *Harnessing GPT-4 so that all students benefit. A nonprofit approach for equal access.* Khan Academy. https://blog.khanacademy.org/harnessing-ai-so-that-all-students-benefit-a-nonprofit-approach-for-equal-access

Kiron, D., & Unruh, G. (2019). Even if AI can cure loneliness-should it?. *MIT Sloan Management Review, 60*(2), 1-4. https://www.proquest.com/openview/a61b93ff9d9855cc06b76a0098c9b15b/1?pq-origsite=gscholar&cbl=26142

Klubnikin, A. (2022). *AI is the new frontier for dating apps.* Here's proof. iTrex. https://itrexgroup.com/blog/ai-for-dating-apps

Kong, S. C., & Zhang, G. (2021). A conceptual framework for designing artificial intelligence literacy programmes for educated citizens. *In Conference proceedings (English paper) of the 25th Global Chinese Conference on Computers in Education (GCCCE 2021)* (pp. 11-15). Centre for Learning, Teaching and Technology, The Education University of Hong Kong.

Kong, S. C., Cheung, W. M. Y., & Zhang, G. (2023). Evaluating an artificial intelligence literacy programme for developing university students' conceptual understanding, literacy, empowerment and ethical awareness. *Educational Technology & Society, 26*(1), 16-30. https://www.jstor.org/stable/pdf/48707964.pdf?casa_token=q2iwmK0-S1kAAAAA:EXpdUbCO2EOODg6TMjWTaX0ZaJfd26W9XFiqhM_UFhbShhIkFgSl4Ik7Vid1_S5DDfxW7avVehiOzD_JsbW7JzNwMaNnjKJA2SgVN8dgNbFzR7x8Zuek

Krishna, K., Song, Y., Karpinska, M., Wieting, J., & Iyyer, M. (2023). Paraphrasing evades detectors of ai-generated text, but retrieval is an effective defense. *arXiv preprint* arXiv:2303.13408. https://arxiv.org/pdf/2303.13408.pdf

Kwok, A. O., & Koh, S. G. (2021). Deepfake: a social construction of technology perspective. *Current Issues in Tourism, 24*(13), 1798-1802. https://www.tandfonline.com/doi/pdf/10.1080/13683500.2020.1738357?casa_token=3npmFqcRTpcAAAAA:_QHhU0FMzwW8acai6ZuQ8usb7m-n5GTRLVcTfgrB6rWsJNwhd_3qSO_gNPQYSBLtOqV0oUOmN4aTJehu

Laird, J. (2023, February 23). Nvidia predicts AI models one million times more powerful than ChatGPT within 10 years. PC Gamer. https://www.pcgamer.com/nvidia-predicts-ai-models-one-million-times-more-powerful-than-chatgpt-within-10-years

Laupichler, M. C., Aster, A., & Raupach, T. (2023). Delphi study for the development and preliminary validation of an item set for the assessment of non-experts' AI literacy. *Computers and Education: Artificial Intelligence, 4,* 100126. https://www.sciencedirect.com/science/article/pii/S266692 0X2300005X

Le, T. T. (2023). Humans befriending their creations: some notes on the human-AI relationship. *Preprint.* 10.31219/osf.io/uyb2p

Loe, M. (2023, March 24). *Heating up: how much energy does AI use?* TechHQ. https://techhq.com/2023/03/data-center-energy-usage-chatgpt

Long, D., & Magerko, B. (2020, April). What is AI literacy? Competencies and design considerations. *Proceedings of the 2020 CHI Conference on Human Factors in Computing systems* (pp. 1-16). https://dl.acm.org/doi/pdf/10.1145/3313831.3376727

Lutkevich, B. (2022). *Language modeling.* Tech Target. https://www.techtarget.com/searchenterpriseai/definitio n/language-modeling

Markowitz, D. (2021). *Transformers, explained: Understand the model behind GPT-3, BERT, and T5*. Dale on AI. https://daleonai.com/transformers-explained

Makridakis, S. (2017). The forthcoming Artificial Intelligence (AI) revolution: Its impact on society and firms. *Futures, 90*, 46-60. https://edisciplinas.usp.br/pluginfile.php/4310583/mod_resource/content/1/The%20forthcoming%20Artificial%20Intelligence%20%28AI%29%20revolution_%20Its%20impact%20on%20society%20and%20firms.pdf

Markovski, Y. (2023). How ChatGPT and our language models are developed. OpenAI. https://help.openai.com/en/articles/7842364-how-chatgpt-and-our-language-models-are-developed

Marr, B. (2019). *The 10 best examples of how companies use artificial intelligence in practice*. Forbes. https://www.forbes.com/sites/bernardmarr/2019/12/09/the-10-best-examples-of-how-companies-use-artificial-intelligence-in-practice/?sh=277475cb7978

Masood, M., Nawaz, M., Malik, K. M., Javed, A., Irtaza, A., & Malik, H. (2023). Deepfakes generation and detection: State-of-the-art, open challenges, countermeasures, and way forward. *Applied Intelligence, 53*(4), 3974-4026. https://arxiv.org/ftp/arxiv/papers/2103/2103.00484.pdf

Mehta, P., Jagatap, G., Gallagher, K., Timmerman, B., Deb, P., Garg, S., Greenstadt, R., & Dolan-Gavitt, B. (2023). Can deepfakes be created by novice users? *ArXiv preprint* arXiv:2304.14576. https://arxiv.org/pdf/2304.14576.pdf

Metz, C. (2023, May 1). 'The Godfather of A.I.' leaves Google and warns of danger ahead. *The New York Times.* https://www.nytimes.com/2023/05/01/technology/ai-google-chatbot-engineer-quits-hinton.html?smid=nytcore-ios-share&referringSource=highlightShare

Microsoft. (2023, May 8). *Is there an age restriction to use the new Bing AI chatbot.* Microsoft. https://answers.microsoft.com/en-us/bing/forum/all/is-there-an-age-restriction-to-use-the-new-bing-ai/a9c22e64-16a3-40a0-9479-30a8e4f4c909

Mills, A. [@EnglishOER]. (2023, May 6). Using GPT-4 to generate sample arguments for students who need to practice recognizing argument structure. It's quite time consuming to [Image attached] [Tweet]. Twitter. https://twitter.com/EnglishOER/status/1654646687787540483

Molad, E., Horwitz, E., Valevski, D., Acha, A. R., Matias, Y., Pritch, Y., ... & Hoshen, Y. (2023). Dreamix: Video diffusion models are general video editors. *arXiv preprint arXiv:*2302.01329. https://arxiv.org/pdf/2302.01329.pdf

Mollick, E. R., & Mollick, L. (2023, May 2). *Unlocking the power of AI: How tools like ChatGPT can make teaching easier and more effective*. Harvard Business Publishing Education: Webinar Recording. https://hbsp.harvard.edu/webinars/unlocking-the-power-of-ai

Mollick, E. R., & Mollick, L. (2023b). Using AI to implement effective teaching strategies in classrooms: Five strategies, including prompts. *Including Prompts*. http://dx.doi.org/10.2139/ssrn.4391243

Moore, S. (2023). *What does ChatGPT mean for healthcare?* News-Medical Life Sciences. https://www.news-medical.net/health/What-does-ChatGPT-mean-for-Healthcare.aspx

Mouriquand, D. (2023, March 23). How AI is putting President Macron at the heart of the French pension protests. *Euronews*. https://www.euronews.com/culture/2023/03/23/how-ai-is-putting-president-macron-at-the-heart-of-the-french-pension-protests

Mukherjee, S., & Vognoni, G. (2023, April 29). *Italy restores ChatGPT after OpenAI responds to regulator*. Reuters. https://www.reuters.com/technology/chatgpt-is-available-again-users-italy-spokesperson-says-2023-04-28

Negishi, M. (2023, April 18). *Japan government to use ChatGPT for first time on red tape*. Bloomberg. https://www.bloomberg.com/news/articles/2023-04-18/japan-government-taps-chatgpt-to-cut-through-bureaucracy-deluge#xj4y7vzkg

Nieweglowska, M., Stellato, C., & Sloman, S. A. (2023). Deepfakes: Vehicles for radicalization, not persuasion. *Current Directions in Psychological Science*, 09637214231161321. https://journals.sagepub.com/doi/pdf/10.1177/09637214231161321?casa_token=OgqzpswpVZ8AAAAA:6zxHdMwg2IsUWUMXcDmVaOR23tPhg2N6GfHZDcz5xXaZKbDx8BGZHVM7g-PrwTDhi7TjnHueNW2ztw

Nori, H., King, N., McKinney, S. M., Carignan, D., & Horvitz, E. (2023). Capabilities of gpt-4 on medical challenge problems. *arXiv preprint* arXiv:2303.13375. https://www.microsoft.com/en-us/research/uploads/prod/2023/03/GPT-4_medical_benchmarks.pdf

Olson, P. (2023, March 24). Fake AI photos are coming to a social network near you. *Washington Post*. https://www.washingtonpost.com/business/2023/03/24/fake-ai-photos-of-macron-and-trump-flood-social-media-expect-more-soon/bce289d6-ca05-11ed-9cc5-a58a4f6d84cd_story.html

OpenAI. (2023, January 8). *About*. OpenAI.

https://openai.com/about

OpenAI. (2023b). GPT-4 technical report. *Arxiv*.

https://arxiv.org/pdf/2303.08774.pdf

OpenAI. (2023c). *Data controls FAQ.* OpenAI.

https://help.openai.com/en/articles/7730893-data-

controls-faq

OpenAI. (2023d). *Text completion.* OpenAI.

https://platform.openai.com/docs/guides/completion/intr

oduction

OpenAI. (2023e). *Terms of Use.* OpenAI.

https://openai.com/policies/terms-of-use

Oracle. (2022). *What is AI? Learn about artificial intelligence.*

Oracle. https://www.oracle.com/artificial-

intelligence/what-is-ai

Pfadenhauer, M., & Lehmann, T. (2021). *Affects after AI:*

Sociological perspectives on artificial companionship. In The

Routledge social science handbook of AI (pp. 91-106).

Routledge.

Parks, M., & Bond, S. (2023, March 26). *AI deepfakes could advance*

misinformation in the run up to the 2024 election. NPR.

https://www.npr.org/2023/03/26/1166114364/ai-

deepfakes-could-advance-misinformation-in-the-run-up-

to-the-2024-election

Passi, S., & Vorvoreanu, M. (2022). Overreliance on AI literature review. *AI Ethics and Effects in Engineering and Research.* https://www.microsoft.com/en-us/research/uploads/prod/2022/06/Aether-Overreliance-on-AI-Review-Final-6.21.22.pdf

Pardes, A. (2019). *This dating app exposes the monstrous bias of algorithms.* Wired. https://www.wired.com/story/monster-match-dating-app

Popli, N. (2023). *The AI job that pays up to $335K—and you don't need a computer engineering background.* Time Magazine. https://time.com/6272103/ai-prompt-engineer-job

Putwain, D. W., Schmitz, E. A., Wood, P., & Pekrun, R. (2021). The role of achievement emotions in primary school mathematics: Control–value antecedents and achievement outcomes. *British Journal of Educational Psychology, 91*(1), 347-367. https://pubmed.ncbi.nlm.nih.gov/32662521

Putwain, D. W., Wood, P., & Pekrun, R. (2020). Achievement emotions and academic achievement: Reciprocal relations and the moderating influence of academic buoyancy. *Journal of Educational Psychology.* https://psycnet.apa.org/doiLanding?doi=10.1037%2Fedu0000637

Quach, K. (2022). University students recruit AI to write essays for them. Now what? *The Register.* https://www.theregister.com/2022/12/27/university_ai_essays_students

Ray, J. (2022). *AI could have 20% chance of sentience in 10 years, says philosopher David Chalmers.* Zdnet. https://www.zdnet.com/article/ai-could-have-20-percent-chance-of-sentience-in-10-years-says-philosopher-david-chalmers

Ridley, M., & Pawlick-Potts, D. (2021). Algorithmic literacy and the role for libraries. *Information technology and libraries*, 40(2). https://ejournals.bc.edu/index.php/ital/article/download/12963/10391

Rivas, S. F., Saiz, C., & Almeida, L. S. (2023). The role of critical thinking in predicting and improving academic performance. *Sustainability, 15*(2), 1527. https://www.mdpi.com/2071-1050/15/2/1527/pdf

Radford, A., Wu, J., Child, R., Luan, D., Amodei, D., & Sutskever, I. (2019). Language models are unsupervised multitask learners. *OpenAI blog, 1*(8), 9. https://cdn.openai.com/better-language-models/language_models_are_unsupervised_multitask_learners.pdf

Robinson, S. (2019, March 26). *The pros and cons of customer service AI*. TechTarget. https://www.techtarget.com/searchcustomerexperience/feature/The-pros-and-cons-of-customer-service-AI

Ruggiero, V. R. (2012). *The art of thinking: A guide to critical and creative thought* (10th ed.). New York, NY: Longman.

Sallam, M., Salim, N., Barakat, M., & Al-Tammemi, A. (2023). ChatGPT applications in medical, dental, pharmacy, and public health education: A descriptive study highlighting the advantages and limitations. *Narra J, 3*(1), e103-e103. https://narraj.org/main/article/download/103/98

Shin, S. Y., & Lee, J. (2022). The effect of deepfake video on news credibility and corrective influence of cost-based knowledge about deepfakes. *Digital Journalism, 10*(3), 412-432. https://www.tandfonline.com/doi/full/10.1080/21670811.2022.2026797

Sky News. (2023). *Joe Biden deepfake responds to questions in 'real-time' using AI*. Sky News Australia [Video]. YouTube. https://youtu.be/DmPDLQNYCbU

Snyder, L. G., & Snyder, M. J. (2008). Teaching critical thinking and problem solving skills. *The Journal of Research in Business Education, 50*(2), 90. http://dme.childrenshospital.org/wp-content/uploads/2019/02/Optional-_Teaching-Critical-Thinking-and-Problem-Solving-Skills.pdf

Sovorel. (2023, February 12). *AI text detection & how to better address the issue* [Video]. YouTube. https://www.youtube.com/watch?v=OBHzraCRqok

Steck, H., Baltrunas, L., Elahi, E., Liang, D., Raimond, Y., & Basilico, J. (2021). Deep learning for recommender systems: A Netflix case study. *AI Magazine, 42*(3), 7-18. https://ojs.aaai.org/index.php/aimagazine/article/view/18140/18876

Sternlicht, A. (2023, May 10). *A 23-year-old Snapchat influencer used OpenAI's technology to create an A.I. version of herself that will be your girlfriend for $1 per minute.* Fortune. https://fortune.com/2023/05/09/snapchat-influencer-launches-carynai-virtual-girlfriend-bot-openai-gpt4

Strauß, S. (2021). " Don't let me be misunderstood": Critical AI literacy for the constructive use of AI technology. *TATuP-Zeitschrift für Technikfolgenabschätzung in Theorie und Praxis/Journal for Technology Assessment in Theory and Practice, 30*(3), 44-49. https://www.ssoar.info/ssoar/bitstream/handle/document/80065/ssoar-tatup-2021-3-strau-Dont_let_me_be_misunderstood.pdf?sequence=1&isAllowed=y&lnkname=ssoar-tatup-2021-3-strau-Dont_let_me_be_misunderstood.pdf

Sudhakar, M. (2023). *How generative AI and ChatGPT are shaping the contact center.* Forbes. https://www.forbes.com/sites/forbestechcouncil/2023/04/10/how-generative-ai-and-chatgpt-are-shaping-the-contact-center/?sh=29f03d621c4b

Sullivan, Y., Nyawa, S., & Fosso Wamba, S. (2023). Combating loneliness with artificial intelligence: An AI-based emotional support model. *Proceedings of the 56th Hawaii International Conference on System Sciences.* https://scholarspace.manoa.hawaii.edu/server/api/core/bitstreams/9498e31c-22c8-42ed-b0c3-0eca9dca85e9/content

Szaniawska-Schiavo, G. (2023). *Love in the age of AI dating apps [2023 Statistics].* Tidio. https://www.tidio.com/blog/ai-dating-apps

TED. (2023, May 1). *The amazing AI super tutor for students and teachers | Sal Khan | TED* [Video]. YouTube. https://youtu.be/hJP5GqnTrNo

Tellez, A. (2023). *These major companies—from Snap to Salesforce— are all using ChatGPT.* Forbes. https://www.forbes.com/sites/anthonytellez/2023/03/03/these-major-companies-from-snap-to-instacart--are-all-using-chatgpt/?sh=612041d84132

Tinmaz, H., Lee, Y. T., Fanea-Ivanovici, M., & Baber, H. (2022). A
systematic review on digital literacy. *Smart Learning
Environments, 9*(1), 1-18.
https://slejournal.springeropen.com/articles/10.1186/s40
561-022-00204-y

Turnitin. (2023). *Turnitin's AI writing detection capabilities.* Turnitin.
https://www.turnitin.com/products/features/ai-writing-
detection

Tyng, C. M., Amin, H. U., Saad, M. N., & Malik, A. S. (2017). The
influences of emotion on learning and memory. *Frontiers in
psychology,* 1454.
https://www.frontiersin.org/articles/10.3389/fpsyg.2017.0
1454/full?fbclid=IwAR1X0KywrVcqD9WOb8KYMIUjlnKMXR
pAwMKUNtEnQoKwxsSFbrzbBzs2tpc

UNESCO. (2022). *UNESCO Forum on AI and education engages
international partners to ensure AI as a common good for
education.* United Nations Educational, Scientific and
Cultural Organization.
https://www.unesco.org/en/articles/unesco-forum-ai-
and-education-engages-international-partners-ensure-ai-
common-good-education

UNESCO. (2023). *UNESCO member states adopt the first ever global agreement on the ethics of AI.* https://www.unesco.org/en/artificial-intelligence/recommendation-ethics

US. (2020). *National AI initiative act of 2020.* Government of the United States of America. https://www.congress.gov/116/crpt/hrpt617/CRPT-116hrpt617.pdf#page=1210

Valero de Urquia, B. (2023). *'Conscious' AI no longer a far-fetched possibility, experts warn.* Engineering and Technology. https://eandt.theiet.org/content/articles/2023/04/conscious-ai-is-no-longer-a-far-fetched-possibility-experts-warn

Vargas-Bianchi, L., Mateus, J. C., Pecho-Ninapaytan, A., & Zambrano-Zuta, S. (2023). 'No, auntie, that's false': Challenges and resources of female baby boomers dealing with fake news on Facebook. *First Monday, Vol28*, N3, doi: https://dx.doi.org/10.5210/fm.v28i3.12678, https://firstmonday.org/article/view/12678/10818

Verdicchio, M., & Perin, A. (2022). When doctors and AI interact: On human responsibility for artificial risks. *Philosophy & technology, 35*(1), 11. https://doi.org/10.1007/s13347-022-00506-6

Voss, A. (2022). *Report on artificial intelligence in a digital age (2020/2266(INI))*. European Parliament: 2019-2024. https://www.europarl.europa.eu/cmsdata/246872/A9-0088_2022_EN.pdf

Wang, B., Rau, P. L. P., & Yuan, T. (2022). Measuring user competence in using artificial intelligence: validity and reliability of artificial intelligence literacy scale. *Behaviour & Information Technology, 1*-14. https://www.researchgate.net/profile/Bingcheng-Wang/publication/360519116_Measuring_user_competence_in_using_artificial_intelligence_validity_and_reliability_of_artificial_intelligence_literacy_scale/links/6408741fb1704f343fb47955/Measuring-user-competence-in-using-artificial-intelligence-validity-and-reliability-of-artificial-intelligence-literacy-scale.pdf

WEF. (2022). *Without universal AI literacy, AI will fail us*. World Economic Forum. https://www.weforum.org/agenda/2022/03/without-universal-ai-literacy-ai-will-fail-us/

Weber, J. (2023, March 23). *Fact check: No, Putin did not kneel before Xi Jinping*. Deutsche Welle (DW), Germany's international broadcaster. https://www.dw.com/en/fact-check-no-putin-did-not-kneel-before-xi-jinping/a-65099092

Weintraub, K. (2023). *ChatGPT is poised to upend medical information. For better and worse.* USA Today. https://www.usatoday.com/story/news/health/2023/02/26/chatgpt-medical-care-doctors/11253952002

Willner, K. (2022). *Class action targeting video interview technology reminds employers of testing risks.* Paul Hastings LLP. https://www.lexology.com/library/detail.aspx?g=5875845a-a613-4014-a72f-7464ba9438a2

Witt, T. (2023, March 10). *Why NLP, ChatGPT require guardrails and content moderation to combat bias.* Acceleration Economy. https://accelerationeconomy.com/ai/why-nlp-chatgpt-require-guardrails-and-content-moderation-to-combat-bias

Wood, P. & Kelly, M. (2023, January 26). 'Everybody is cheating': Why this teacher has adopted an open ChatGPT policy. NPR. https://www.npr.org/2023/01/26/1151499213/chatgpt-ai-education-cheating-classroom-wharton-school

Wolfe, M. (2023, January 23). Using AI to generate text-to-video! Things are moving fast [Video]. YouTube. https://youtu.be/6aHMepbNkmE

Yang, W. (2022). Artificial Intelligence education for young children: Why, what, and how in curriculum design and implementation. *Computers and Education: Artificial Intelligence, 3*, 100061. https://www.sciencedirect.com/science/article/pii/S2666920X22000169

Yeung, J., & Maruyama, M. (2023, April 21). *As Japan's population drops, one city is turning to ChatGPT to help run the government.* CNN. https://edition.cnn.com/2023/04/21/asia/japan-yokosuka-government-chatgpt-intl-hnk/index.html

You. (2023). *Privacy policy: How we use the information we collect in standard mode.* You.com. https://you.com/legal/privacy

Zaichenko, D. (2023). *11 artificial intelligence issues you should worry about in 2023.* Coupler.io. https://blog.coupler.io/artificial-intelligence-issues/#AI_will_replace_humans_in_many_jobs

Zarifhonarvar, A. (2023). Economics of chatgpt: A labor market view on the occupational impact of artificial intelligence. *SSRN* 4350925. https://www.econstor.eu/handle/10419/268826

Zhou, Z. (2023, April 14). Evaluation of ChatGPT's capabilities in medical report generation. *Cureus 15*(4): e37589. doi:10.7759/cureus.37589. https://www.cureus.com/articles/143224-evaluation-of-chatgpts-capabilities-in-medical-report-generation#!

About the Author

Brent A. Anders, PhD., has worked in higher education for over twenty years, concentrating on education, digital media, communication, student interaction, online instruction, and other instructional technologies. Anders has extensively worked as an educational media consultant (video production, live webcasting, and student experience/engagement), a course developer/instructional designer, web accessibility advisor, educational author, and a lecturer. Anders also served in the U.S. Army for over 25 years, first as an airborne infantryman, then as an international certificated military instructor with additional leadership positions. Anders personally trained hundreds of soldiers all over the world, retiring as a Sergeant Major while working with the U.S. Embassy in Armenia as part of the Kansas Army National Guard State Partnership Program.

Anders currently works at a major university in Armenia, (The American University of Armenia), as the Director of Institutional Research and Assessment, and the Center for Teaching and Learning, as well as a Lecturer. His work involves helping professors and other instructors develop professionally in their instructional capabilities. Additionally, Anders directly works with the university Provost in the development of new policies and processes to help ensure effective management and improvement of the educational experience for faculty, staff, and students.

Anders authors books and research articles (focusing on education to include instructional technology such as AI and general faculty/student development), does periodic international speaking events, and hosts a dedicated educational YouTube channel (https://www.youtube.com/@sovorel-EDU and educational blog: www.sovorelpublishing.com For a full listing of Brent A. Anders' academic publications please visit https://aua.academia.edu/BrentAnders

⁇

Feedback

Thank you very much for reading this special book. I hope it will directly help you to understand and develop AI Literacy as well as to see its extreme importance in the new world around us. If the information was helpful to you in any way, I would greatly appreciate a favorable review on Amazon.

If you would like to contact me directly, please message me on Twitter (**https://twitter.com/BrentAAnders**) or use the contact form at Sovorel Publishing: **www.sovorelpublishing.com** or **contact@sovorelpublishing.com**

www.sovorelpublishing.com

Other Available Books

ChatGPT AI in Education: What it is and how to Use it in the Classroom, available on Amazon:
https://www.amazon.com/ChatGPT-AI-Education-What-Classroom/dp/B0BRLT8ZMF

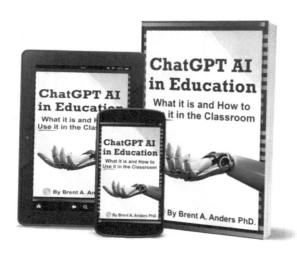

This book provides an easy-to-understand explanation of what ChatGPT is and, more importantly, how to use it in many different ways within the classroom. Each of the many implementations is explained with examples of the prompts used and a discussion of the many benefits provided. The detailed examples and instructions described will allow you to quickly increase your AI literacy and help you better develop your student AI literacy while working with ChatGPT and harnessing its many capabilities.

Additional useful information is presented regarding ethical considerations, the future of education, and what might be next regarding AI and ChatGPT. A glossary of terms, references to the many citations used, and a listing of additional resources are also provided.

How to Be a Super Student: Based on Science and Experience,
available on Amazon: https://www.amazon.com/How-Be-Super-Student-Experience/dp/0998763756

This powerful book unlocks all the secrets to truly being a Super Student. Professor and life-long learner Brent A. Anders, PhD., provides key insights from his many educational experiences both in higher education and as a retired military instructor, along with reflections made by his many students, and information learned from cutting-edge learning science research. Each one of the key concepts presented manifests as a new academic superpower to help ensure that you will thrive and succeed in all your academic pursuits.

Seven Characteristics of an Excellent Instructor: Based on Learning Science, available on Amazon: https://www.amazon.com/Characteristics-Excellent-Instructor-Learning-Science-ebook/dp/B0839CXTLQ

This highly useful compact e-book presents the top seven characteristics of excellent instructors derived from over 50 scientific journals and resources (from 2000 to 2020).

Each characteristic is fully described, explained, and suggestions on how to develop these characteristics are provided to help all educational practitioners improve and become excellent instructors.

The Army Learning Concept, Army Learning Model: A Guide to Understanding and Implementation, available on Amazon: https://www.amazon.com/Army-Learning-Concept-Model-Implementation/dp/0998763721

This book is a powerful implementation guide to fully use and integrate the benefits of the Army Learning Concept (ALC), Army Learning Model (ALM).

Areas covered include improving interaction via enhanced instructional presence, enhanced instructional techniques and technologies such as virtual reality, reaching adult learners, Gen Zs, and everything in between. ⯑

How to Enhance Instructional Presence, available on Amazon:
https://www.amazon.com/gp/product/0998763713

This book deals with how to specifically make students feel more like a real learning member of an instructional community (of inquiry) and not "just a number."

The book describes how strategic implementations of video can be used to enhance social, cognitive, and teaching presence to maximize instructional effectiveness, engagement, instructor approachableness, student achievement, and improve educational experiences.

?

Take a Walk with Me: How to Develop GRIT, a True Story

Soon to be available on Amazon (www.amazon.com). "Take a Walk with Me" will deal with the very important topic of grit. It is an interesting type of book because it presents grit through the lens of a true story about completing a 15-mile road march in the Army. It then breaks grit down into easy-to-understand components along with ways to develop grit within your own life.

"Take a Walk with Me" will provide a deep emotional understanding along with scientific references, all to create a roadmap to success. The power of grit is that it helps us succeed in learning, health/fitness, business, relationships, and all aspects of life. It is a vital component in helping us achieve our goals and true purpose in life.

Thank you for your support.

www.sovorelpublishing.com